Our Enduring Values

Librarianship in the 21st Century

Michael Gorman

AMERICAN LIBRARY ASSOCIATION
Chicago and London
2000

Text and cover design by Dianne M. Rooney

Composition by the dotted i in Avant Garde and Minion using QuarkXPress 4.0 on a Macintosh

Printed on 50-pound white offset, a pH-neutral stock, and bound in 10-point cover stock by McNaughton & Gunn

The paper used in this publication meets the minimum requirements of American National Standard for Information Sciences—Permanence of Paper for Printed Library Materials, ANSI Z39.48-1992. ∞

Library of Congress Cataloging-in-Publication Data

Gorman, Michael, 1941–
    Our enduring values : librarianship in the 21st century / by Michael Gorman.
      p.   cm.
    Includes index.
    ISBN 0-8389-0785-7 (alk. paper)
    1. Libraries—Aims and objectives—United States. 2. Library science—Moral and ethical aspects—United States. 3. Librarians—Professional ethics—United States
    I. Title.
    Z716.4.G67   2000
    027—dc21   00-027127

Printed in the United States of America.

04   03   5   4   3   2

This book is dedicated to

Katherine Hepburn and Spencer Tracy,

the stars,

and

Phoebe and Harold Ephron,

the writers

of

Desk Set,

the definitive "information science" movie

CONTENTS

PREFACE

The World Turned Upside Down?

Though it was to be two years before a formal peace was signed, the surrender of Lord Cornwallis in October 1781 at Yorktown, Virginia, marked the successful close of the American Revolution. It was the day on which the independence of the United States was assured. On the 19th of October, after a heated discussion of the terms of surrender, the defeated British and German troops "marched out with colors cased, while the tune they chose to follow was the old British march with the quite appropriate title of 'The world turned upside down.'"[1]

There are those who believe that an electronic Yorktown lies in the future of libraries, that the widespread use of electronic communication is as revolutionary a force as the Revolutionary allied army of Americans and French, and that, sooner rather than later, the garrison of the traditional library will fall, leaving librarians to steal from the scene—their world turned upside down. The question, of course, is whether libraries will be destroyed or strengthened by that technology. Is the Virtual Library at war with the traditional library or is it possible that what we are experiencing is not a revolution and certainly not a war? I am convinced that the "digital revolution," "the Age of Information," and all the other phrases that are common today are hollow metaphors and take us away from the direction in which we should be going—the direction of incorporation, cooperation, coexistence, and peaceful progress. The only metaphorical war I know of in this arena is the war over the allocation of funds between traditional library resources and information technology. That is an important struggle and one with real consequences, but it is a matter neither of high principle nor of philosophical consequence. As noted earlier, there are still people who believe or purport to believe that electronic technology will drive out all other forms of recording, disseminating, and preserving knowledge and information, and, in so doing, transform education, learning, leisure, and the nature of society. It seems obvious to most, however, that such a revolution is not happening and will not happen and that libraries will continue to incorporate electronic technology into all their programs and services, thus enhancing the service that we render to society. The former is a narrow, almost totalitarian, point of view. The latter is a vision of evolution, enhancement, growth, and progress.

NOTE

1. Henry P. Johnston, *The Yorktown Campaign and the Surrender of Cornwallis* (New York: Harper, 1881), 155.

ACKNOWLEDGMENTS

I wish to acknowledge the help of Marlene Chamberlain and Mary Huchting of ALA Editions at all stages of this book. Dave Tyckoson, my colleague at Fresno State, has supplied me with many ideas, as have a number of other colleagues in this library. I am grateful for discussions on a variety of topics with Susan Curzon, Marion Reid, and Jim Schmidt, fellow members of the California State University Council of Library Directors. My assistant, Susan Mangini, has been her invariably invaluable, conscientious, and thoughtful self. I owe a debt to countless professional colleagues who, I trust, know who they are and how much I value their ideas and friendship.

As ever, I am eternally grateful for the love and support of my daughters, Emma and Alice.

Introduction

Why write or expect anyone to read a book on library values? The answer is quite simple. We live and work in a time of change. Old certainties no longer seem to apply, and many librarians are fearful about the future of libraries and of our profession. For example, a recent widely publicized discussion of library education seems to have encountered great difficulty in dealing with divisions between librarians and library educators.[1] Those divisions betray a lack of consensus about common beliefs and values and, often, completely different predictions about the future. What I seek to do, and what, dear reader, I hope you will find in this book, is to illuminate and re-create the underpinnings of our profession to, at least, provide a framework for discussion and, at best, be a broad plan with which we may all proceed.

People intensify the search for meaning in life in an age of prosperity. Once the basic needs—food, housing, education, health—are paid for and secure, that search is on at all levels. Religion, from its most demanding manifestations to undemanding and vaguely defined "spirituality," is not an escape from the rigors of life for the prosperous but an enhancement for those who have come to realize that the material world is not enough. Other religious revivals come about in an age of massive change—times in which the enjoyment of the present is mitigated by unformulated fear of the future. Outside religion, individuals and groups seek the ethics and determining beliefs that define them as soon as they get beyond the struggle for mere survival. In a sense, the world of libraries is a microcosm of the wider world—buoyed by technology but daunted by the unknown, changing in ways that most of us understand dimly, if at all. It is a world in which the economic bases of libraries and the products in which we deal are subject to unpredictable forces. A world of in-group jargon, constant change, new demands for new services, and the inexplicable, omnipresent, queasy sense of the ground shifting beneath our feet—all these apply to our work in libraries and to the wider world in which we live and which our libraries serve.

We must understand and weigh that wider context if we are to understand and make coherent the working world of libraries. Libraries, library services, and librarianship are caught in a process of seemingly constant change—change that is almost universally ascribed to technology. It would be a mistake, though, either to see libraries as a self-contained system or to praise (or blame) technology for everything. The technological changes that we have seen in libraries over the past twenty-five years have been dramatic, but they pale in comparison to parallel changes in society, politics, lifestyles, and almost every other aspect of human life. If we think that the impact of automation in libraries, the Internet, and the World Wide Web has been profound, we should step back for a moment and compare it to the impact created by the following:

> the globalization of trade
>
> the creation of an interdependent world economy
>
> the fall of communism in Eastern Europe and the transformation for good and ill of the societies of that region
>
> advances in medicine that have increased life spans in developed countries and led to the aging of the population
>
> the success of the women's movement in developed democracies
>
> the rise of Asian democracy and economic power
>
> the end of the Cold War
>
> the advent of global news companies, such as CNN
>
> the rise in the amount and types of leisure in the developed world
>
> a parallel increase in famine and deprivation in the developing and underdeveloped worlds
>
> the negative impact of fossil fuels and industrialization on the world's environment
>
> the rise of fundamentalism across the world
>
> the change from industrialization to service economies in the developed world
>
> the devolution of industrialization from the developed to the developing world
>
> the conflict in all societies between "globalization" and "social atavism"
>
> the rise in global terrorism

These and many other trends are influenced by technology, of course, and, in many cases, intertwined with it. Global trade is clearly linked to the rise of global information sharing and instantaneous news. The change from industrialized economies to service economies in the developed world is technology driven. Other kinds of change (environmental, social, and so on) are, in many cases, affected by technology but have other, deeper roots. To take but one example, the conflict over whether libraries should restrict children's access to electronic resources by filtering or other means clearly centers on technology. Equally clearly, it is a manifestation of the clash between different social and political attitudes that predates modern technology by decades, if not centuries.

It is impossible to separate any of the trends and events in the preceding list from all the others, and the impact of technology on libraries is a microcosm of the impact of technology on the whole world. It is important to note that we, as human beings, are part of the society in which we live and that society is part of an increasingly interconnected network that constitutes, potentially, an emerging global society. We must always bear in mind that what is happening to libraries is a result of what is happening to social life, social organization, and global economic trends.

Le plus ça change . . .

Literature from any period shows that the people of that time believed that they were living in an era of unprecedented change. It is ever so, and current change is always more fraught than past change, for the simple reason that we know the results of past change but have no means of foreseeing the results of the changes that are happening or forecast now. However you look at it, change *is* happening, and more change is coming. There are two ways to deal with certain change. One is to be passive and reflexive, allowing whatever happens to happen. The other is to plan for and, insofar as is possible, to control change. This is not a book on planning—there is an ample sufficiency of those—but a book that urges consideration of the values that underlie our work in libraries and as librarians, because planning can never be effective in the absence of intellectual and philosophical underpinning. Human beings need a rationale for all their activities because it is that rationale that raises activities above drudgery and lifts human lives to a higher level. This is not to advocate the veiling of burdensome toil or the sanctification of unnecessary labor, but the power of service and other values to validate useful work. I imagine that, in our hearts, all we librarians know that what we do is useful and good and that the cumulation of all our useful and good working lives is far greater than the sum of its parts. However, in my experience of more than forty years in libraries, there are now more librarians who question what they do—the very underpinnings of their working lives—than ever before. Two words account for this phenomenon—change and uncertainty.

Values and Value

In every aspect of our lives, we live in an age of uncertainty. Despite the economic prosperity of most of the 1990s and the end of the Cold War, most of us, though happy enough with our present circumstances, fear the changes we see and, even more, the changes yet to come. This uncertainty pervades our working lives. Controversy swirls around the future of librarianship and libraries and it is difficult to deal with the various futures that are foreseen by pundits, especially as most of them seem to question the very existence of our profession. The discontinuity between working librarians and library users on the one hand and academic theorists, "information scientists," many library educators, and some of the leaders of our profession on the other becomes ever more obvious. The first group laments declining materials budgets; run-down, overcrowded libraries; and the terrible pressures of always doing more with less. At more or less the same time, the second group publishes incomprehensible papers about digital libraries, issues fantastical reports (like the execrable *Benton Report*[2]), holds conferences that float on an abundant supply of hot air, and generally basks in the delights of shooting the rest of us in the foot. The gap between the elitists and the workers in, and users of, libraries has never been greater. That gap is attributable, almost entirely, to the fact that those interested in libraries but not concerned with libraries on a day-to-day basis are far more likely to be enthusiastic about virtual libraries than those who deal daily with the realities of modern libraries and their use. Those of us who believe in real libraries serving real people need, now more than ever, to reaffirm our values and value. To do that, we must understand the nature of values and come to terms with library values and their application.

Adventures in Axiology

Axiology	Pronunciation:	ak-sE-ˈä-lə-jE
	Function:	noun
	Etymology:	Greek *axios* + International Scientific Vocabulary *-logy*
	Date:	1908

The study of the nature, types, and criteria of values and of value judgments especially in ethics.[3]

A *value* is something that is of deep interest (often and quite reasonably self-interest) to an individual or a group. When a group of values is assembled, they form a "value system." We speak of values in a variety of contexts: economic, moral, religious, artistic, scientific, political, professional, and legal. In each of these spheres, the term has a different though related meaning. The simplest and most widely understood is the economic definition, though even here the concept of "value" is nowhere near as measurable as that of price, even though it is far more important and enduring. In other fields, one only has to think of such terms as "artistic value" (in an age when a cow in formaldehyde wins a major art prize) and "political values" (in an age in which political parties are wholly owned subsidiaries of commercial and other interests) to realize what a slippery word "value" is. It is important to recognize the role of self-interest in the formulation of values because even the most altruistic values can be interpreted as a reasonable person or group of reasonable people pursuing courses of action or states of existence that benefit them. For example, two core Western values are the freedom of the individual and the well-being of society (the greater good). A sensible person will realize, first, that these values are, inescapably, in conflict and must constantly be weighed one against the other; and, second, that though freedom of the individual obviously benefits the individual, so does the greater good. After all, only a nihilist or extreme libertarian would reject a harmonious community delivering the greater good to all its members. In other words, values are rooted in realities and do not exist in and of themselves as philosophical entities. Each group and each generation must establish its values, retaining those that remain of interest and self-interest, discarding those that no longer apply, and creating new values or, more likely, reinterpretations of old values.

Here is one of the more concise definitions of "value":

> A value is an enduring belief that a specific mode of conduct or end-state of existence is personally or socially preferable to an opposite or converse mode of conduct or end-state of existence. A value system is an enduring organization of beliefs concerning preferable modes of conduct or end-states of existence along a continuum of relative importance.[4]

This definition has several points of interest. The first is that the author equates values and beliefs. Later, he defines different classes of belief and says that values belong to the class of what he calls prescriptive beliefs—that is, those that make judgments about what is or is not desirable about certain conduct or ways of being. To say, for example, that democracy is a core value of librarianship implies the preceding statement, "I believe in democracy and think it is the best political system I know." You will note here that such beliefs and the values founded on those beliefs are personal in essence; the individual has to believe and hold a value before she or he can associate with others who hold the same values to form a community of interest.

Second, note that the definition states that a value is also a preference. That is, in embracing a value, one is implicitly rejecting antitheses and alternatives. If your library value is service, you are inherently rejecting the concept of the library of value apart from its use by library patrons (which used to be a common view of many research libraries), and you are rejecting a lack of service orientation.

The third interesting point is in the word "enduring." The definition makes it plain that values have to have a long life and be capable of being as valid in three decades as they are today and were three decades ago. A value, to be of use, must animate its adherents' actions and existence over a long period. This is not to say that values are, by definition, absolutely immutable. Anything, including anything in the realm of ideas and beliefs, may change. If a belief is to rise to the level of a value, such change must be gradual and evolutionary and should concern shades of meaning rather than the core of the value itself. In my opinion, a value, once arrived at, should be fixed enough to provide continuity of thought and action but flexible enough to allow a person or group to reassign priorities because of change in circumstances or ideas.

The fourth point of interest is that the definition explicitly refers to matters of conduct and to end-states of existence—in short, to both means and ends. Let me take *stewardship*—a library value to which I will return—as an example. In being stewards of our collections, our conduct is that of preserving recorded knowledge and information in all its forms, and the end-state that value wishes to achieve is that the people of the future will be able to know what we know. The means are selection and preservation techniques of various kinds and the end is the transmittal of the records of humankind to posterity. Some thinkers, notably John Dewey, have tried to show that the difference between an instrumental value (what is good as a course of conduct) and an intrinsic value (what is good as a desired state of existence) is not of any great philosophical importance. Others contend that there is an important difference between these kinds of values and go so far as to create subcategories of ends and means. As far as libraries are concerned, this seems to me a distinction with very little difference in application. Many of the values that I will discuss later are both means and ends. We should follow the wise injunction to "be what you want to become." In, for example, carrying out library service, one is achieving library service, and the central value of service is, thus, both a means and an end.[5]

Why Values?

In application, values are useful and usable because they are standards by which we can assess what we do; measure how near we are to, or how far we are from, an objective; and compare our actions and our state of being to those of others and to the ideals represented by our values. Values also provide a basis for argument and discussion and a set of premises needed for fruitful interaction with other people and with other groups. In addition to their usefulness as yardsticks to measure our conduct, goals, and ways of life, values are also psychologically important to individuals and groups. If you are secure in your value system and the beliefs of which it is comprised, then even failure is bearable because your values tell you that what you did was worthwhile and the end you were trying to achieve was honorable. A person secure in her or his values is likely to have robust self-esteem, at least in the sphere of action or being to which those values apply.

There is, of course, a dark side. Values may be sincerely held but also have moved beyond preference to become *absolutes*. In such distorted value systems, an adherent is always and unshakably right, and those with other beliefs and preferences are viewed as not merely different or not merely wrong but evil. This is the stuff of intolerance and religious wars. One of the most dangerous delusions of the modern age is the Romantic idea that sincerity is always admirable in itself. The world is full of sincere bigots so consumed by the rightness of their value systems that they use any means to impose them on others. If anything, sincerity harnessed to a desire to impose your values on others is far more anti-social than the deepest cynicism. It is of this that book-banners, clinic bombers, brainwashers, and totalitarians and tyrants of all kinds are made. There are, then, "good" values and, at least potentially, "bad" values.

What are the characteristics of "good" values? This question assumes a kind of metavalue or set of metavalues by which we can express preferences and beliefs about values that, in turn, govern our actions and being. Our society is founded, at least nominally, on the metavalues of reason and tolerance as opposed to conformity of faith and intolerance. Religious people are fond of the direction to "love the sinner and hate the sin." Sin, of course, is a matter of faith, and, on examination, that direction translates as: Love other human beings but hate their conduct if it is outside the norms in which *I* believe. Leaving aside the universal proscriptions of murder, violent robbery, and the like (while noting that such things are universally forbidden but all too frequently practiced), the sins of one belief system may be nothing of the sort to those who adhere to other belief systems or to none at all. A modern, pluralistic society, particularly one in which individual rights are codified in laws or constitutions, is, by definition, a society of tolerance and understanding. A value is not "good" just because you or I agree with it any more than a value is "bad" because we do not. This is not a battleground of belief and ideas but a way of looking at life and work that seeks positive common ground and the essentials of a profession that is dedicated to serving humankind.

As a prelude to the discussion of specific values and their application, let us define our working environment and our work as librarians.

What Is a Library?

Many years ago, there was a simple answer to that question. A library was a building or rooms set apart to house books and other printed materials and make them available for study. That simple definition not only does not fit now, but also has not fit for decades. The word "library" is a concept that embraces library service, library collections, library staff, and a range of activities that take place inside and outside the physical plant that is the most visible manifestation of the concept "library." Consider for a moment the CD-ROMs that the Library of Congress has made of many of its archival collections in order to give access to unique and fragile materials to anyone with a computer. Is it unreasonable to say that, for people using those CD-ROMs in Spokane, Edinburgh, and St. Petersburg, the Library of Congress is manifest in Washington State, Scotland, and Russia as much as it is in the stately buildings in Washington, D.C.? A library's Web page may seem to be the very summit of the globally ubiquitous library, but is it qualitatively different from the published library catalogues of the past? My point is that modern technology has made more efficient and widespread access to library resources and collections much more possible than in the past. Those facts do not mean that we are dealing with an entirely new concept of the "library." The results of modern technology are by no means the first manifestation of libraries making their presence felt far beyond the walls of their buildings.

More than forty years ago, I worked in a large public library in London that had a number of branches, two mobile libraries, and an active service to the house-bound and the hospitalized. Its collections included books, periodicals, microforms, paintings and prints, maps, sound recordings, scores, films, toys, and puppets—all of which were available to be borrowed. The great technological innovation was a circulation system called "photocharging," which involved microfilm and punched cards and speeded the circulation process greatly. The proportion of residents registered with the public library was well above 50 percent. I am not describing this library as an exercise in nostalgia but to indicate that there is nothing new about the idea of a library as an omnipresent force in its community that transcends its buildings, uses current technology, and collects and gives access to materials in all formats. Put another way, if a time-traveling Connecticut Yankee were to go from 2000 to that library in 1958 to install an online system and give access to the Web and the Net across the years, would the difference be transcendent or just a matter of degree? Further, if those modern wonders had to be paid for by running down some of the excellent services of 1958, would the overall difference be for the better or the worse? I bring up this example and fanciful notion simply to raise some difficult questions and challenge some of the received wisdom of today. I certainly do not believe that time and its effects can be reversed, and would not wish to do so if they could. Modern technology has many advantages and many features that can enhance library service. However, library technology needs to be considered coolly and rationally and fitted into the history and evolution of libraries, rather than greeted as an unqualified blessing, still less as a technoquake leveling the very idea of libraries to create a new and radically different cyber-entity.

What Is Librarianship?

Long ago, people wrote about something called "library economy," a term that stresses the practical, results-oriented nature of our profession. Later, Ranganathan coined the term "library science," a term that embodied his idea that librarianship could be thought of in terms of scientific principles that governed all the activities of librarians. Today, both seem to be old-fashioned terms, as indeed does "librarianship," but what are we to use in its place? Whatever the term, we need to understand what librarians do and the corpus of knowledge shared by librarians if we are to discuss our values and philosophy. The lack of a commonly accepted definition of librarianship is not new. Jesse Shera wrote:

> [L]ibrarianship, unfortunately, has been little given to professional introspection. For generations, librarians have accepted the social responsibility for custody of mankind's graphic records, hammered out empirical procedures for the organization and servicing, and argued indifferently the right of their technology to qualify as a science.[6]

Chapter 1 deals with philosophy and theory and the lack of them in librarianship, so here I will content myself with the empirical task of defining the work of the librarian in terms of what she or he does and has done for generations.

Before I do that, I would like to advance a modern definition of the word "collection." Even in times past, this seemingly innocuous word was capable of interpretation. For example, did all the books held by a library with many branches constitute a collection or a number of collections? This might seem to be an insignificant point, but the answer to that question has ramifications for library administration, cataloguing, and collection development. If such an aggregation is viewed as comprising a number of collections, then each should have its own collection development policy. It follows that those policies will be different one from the other and might demand different funding based on the needs of the clientele of each branch. If, on the other hand, the aggregation is regarded as one collection, the library will have one collection development policy and centralized funding. In that case, the needs of the wider community served by the unified library may well be satisfied to the detriment of the clientele of the individual branches. The idea of the "collection" was further complicated by the growth and use of union catalogues, by means of which the collection of one library was made available to the clientele of others. Then, those complications were multiplied by the advent of electronic resources. For some time, those resources were not only not viewed as part of the library's collections, but were even paid for from sources other than the budget for library materials. That is still the case in many libraries—if you follow the money, you have to conclude that electronic resources are not seen as part of the library's collections. That practice is mistaken for financial and strategic reasons, but it is also conceptually flawed.

In my view, the "collection" of a modern library includes the following:

> tangible objects (books, and so on) that the library owns
>
> local intangible (electronic) resources owned and controlled by the library (CD-ROMs, and the like)
>
> tangible objects owned by other libraries, but accessible to local patrons by means of union catalogues and interlibrary lending schemes
>
> remote intangible resources not owned by the library but to which the library gives access

Given that definition of a collection, it is easy to become carried away by the metaphor of concentric circles (beginning with the "traditional" collection of the local library) that expand endlessly to comprehend all the recorded knowledge and information in the world. A good antidote to that hyperbolic concept is to remember that most library patrons prefer local resources that they can have and use immediately. That is even truer when you are dealing with good local collections built over many years with the needs of the local community in mind and supplemented by easily available electronic resources used with caution.

With that expanded definition of a collection as the backdrop, this is what librarians do:

Select

> tangible objects (books, printed journals, scores, recorded sound, films and videos, manuscripts, microforms, etc.) to be added to the library's collection
>
> by creating profiles that define the kinds of material to be acquired by the library through gathering (approval) plans
>
> electronic resources to be purchased *or* subscribed to *or* identified as part of the library's service to its users

Acquire

> by purchase (either by individual order or through gathering plans)
>
> by subscription (journals, electronic resources, etc.)
>
> by gift and exchange mechanisms

Organize and give access

by cataloguing according to national and international standards

by classifying library materials in order to organize tangible objects *or* to facilitate subject retrieval in online systems *or* both

by creating and maintaining online systems

by adding cataloguing records to national databases and union catalogues

by maintaining the library's physical collections

Preserve and conserve

by using good conservation techniques to ensure that tangible collections are passed on to future users in the best possible condition

by working cooperatively with other libraries to ensure the survival of "last copies"

by working with others to preserve electronic documents and resources of value

by medium-specific preservation policies, such as transferring 35-mm films to video formats, conserving archives, and copying fragile documents to CD-ROMs to reduce or eliminate handling

Assist library users

by maintaining and giving good, accessible general reference service to all library users

by creating and maintaining user-friendly systems and environments conducive to easy use of the range of library materials

by making the library's collections accessible with the minimum necessary effort on the part of the users

by creating and making available guides to library use in all formats (print, Web pages, etc.)

Instruct library users

by devising and implementing instruction programs that teach

- basic library skills
- basic computer skills
- how to locate, identify, and use relevant sources

- how to choose the format(s) most likely to yield relevant answers to specific questions
- critical thinking

by incorporating instruction in the preceding skills into reference service in environments in which formal instruction programs are either infeasible or inappropriate

by using all available modern pedagogical techniques to carry on instruction programs

Administer and manage the library and its personnel, services, and programs

There are few, if any, libraries in which librarians do, or should do, all aspects of all the tasks listed here. In the vast majority of libraries, librarians work with paraprofessional and clerical library workers and with professionals in other areas (systems, personnel, etc.) to accomplish everything that is part of the library's mission. Once the basic tasks are delineated, the next step is to define the professional quotient of each task. That delineation is not because that quotient is superior to the rest of the activities, but simply to deploy the library's (usually) limited professional human resources in the places in which they can do most good. Circumstances vary from library to library but, in general, these are the professional components of library work:

creating and monitoring collection development policies

creating and monitoring profiles for gathering plans

managing acquisitions activities

performing original cataloguing and classification

performing archival and special collections cataloguing

performing systems work*

devising and managing conservation and preservation policies

performing general and specialized reference service

devising, managing, and delivering instruction programs

leading, administering, and managing the library*

managing human resources (personnel)* and budgeting*

fund-raising*

There is a continuing debate of some years standing about whether one needs to be a librarian to carry out the tasks marked with an asterisk (*). I am convinced, from observation of American libraries headed by nonlibrarians, that librarians make the best heads of libraries. This is not to say that all librarians possess the necessary good hearts and organized minds that define good library leaders, but those who do possess those desirable characteristics *and* the training and experience make very good library leaders indeed. This observation is reinforced by the experience of academic libraries in continental Europe and Asia, which are almost invariably headed by nonlibrarian academics. That is one of the main reasons those libraries are vastly inferior to their professionally led American counterparts.

Given the choice between a librarian with good systems experience and background and a systems person with a little library learning, I would choose the former any time. The same goes for librarian fund-raisers. On the other hand, I think professionally trained personnel and budget/finance officers may best serve a library that is large enough to need such specialists.

What Is a Librarian?

The empirical answer to that question is: a person who, after receiving a master's-level education at an accredited school and on-the-job training, carries out one or more of the tasks listed earlier. There are, of course, other dimensions to being a librarian, such as new tasks occurring in new or specialized contexts, activity in professional associations, continuing education, and research and publication. If a librarian creates Web pages to further reference service or library instruction, that creation becomes a professional activity. If a librarian uses the skills she has acquired in creating Web pages for professional purposes to become a "Webmaster" (in the current sexist, neo-Tolkienish jargon) for a university, company, or community, then her work may be worthwhile but it is not librarianship. The point is that the tasks of the librarian do not change, but the means and processes we use to accomplish those tasks can, should, and will change. Further, the mission of the library today and the broad tasks of the librarian have far more in common with the libraries and librarians of the nineteenth century than they do with a computer center. The waning 1980s fad for combining libraries and computer centers on the basis that they are both concerned with "information" is waning precisely because the premise for those mergers was, and proved to be, unsustainable. Libraries are different from other entities, librarianship has a structure and a history, and it behooves librarians to recognize and celebrate their unique identity and mission.

Now that we have looked at what modern libraries are and what modern librarians do, let us consider the history of the philosophy and basic ideas of librarianship in the nineteenth and twentieth centuries . . .

NOTES

1. ALA's Congress on Professional Education, Washington, D.C., April 1999.

2. *Buildings, Books, and Bytes: Libraries and Communities in the Digital Age* (Washington, D.C.: Benton Foundation, 1996). See also Michael Gorman, "Living and Dying with 'Information,'" *Library Trends* 46, no. 1 (summer 1997): 28–35.

3. WWWebster dictionary (Springfield, Mass.: Meriam Webster). *www.m-w.com/cgi-bin/dictionary*

4. Milton Rokeach, *The Nature of Human Values* (New York: Free Press, 1973).

5. This discussion of Rokeach's definition is based on the explication in Norman T. Feather, *Values in Education and Society* (New York: Free Press, 1975), 4.

6. Jesse H. Shera, *Libraries and the Organization of Knowledge* (London: Crosby, Lockwood; Hamden, Conn.: Archon, 1965), 162–163.

1

The History
and Philosophy
of Library Values

A Distrust of Philosophy?

Throughout library history, from the Sumerians of the third millennium before the Common Era to today's many faces of libraries, librarianship has been seen as intensely practical. As late as 1933, Pierce Butler wrote:

> Unlike his colleagues in other fields of social activity, the librarian is strangely uninterested in the theoretical aspects of his profession. . . . The librarian apparently stands alone in the simplicity of his pragmatism; a rationalization of each immediate process by itself seems to satisfy his intellectual interest. Indeed, any endeavor to generalize these rationalizations into a professional philosophy appears to him not merely futile but positively dangerous.[1]

Butler was embarking on a plea for the scientific method in librarianship and, in the manner of writers at all times, here overstates the opposite position. However, it is no coincidence that many of the towering figures of the founding years of modern librarianship were, essentially, doers rather than thinkers. For all of Melvil Dewey's philosophical underpinnings for his Decimal classification (Aristotle and all that), he was primarily concerned with arranging books on shelves. Antonio Panizzi's whole career was one of overachievement and bustle—the quintessential Victorian man of action. There is a literature of the philosophy of librarianship and there are some important library thinkers (notably Jesse Shera and S. R. Ranganathan), but most achievements in librarianship are the result of problem solving and the pragmatic approach. Even the more cerebral areas of librarianship—cataloguing and classification—

turn out, on examination, to be based on theories that almost always have been developed after the event or by accretion of cases. (Ranganathan and Lubetzky are shining exceptions to this rule.)

We are, then, dealing with a profession that has evolved over many centuries without too much regard to philosophy, overarching principles, and values, but with great respect for the practical, the useful, and the utilitarian. One could almost say that we have evolved a kind of antiphilosophy of practicality—one that values what works and discards what does not. I hardly need to point out that utilitarianism is itself a philosophy—one that finds morality in the greatest good of the greatest number. One can be a perfectly good librarian if one acts on utilitarian principles. For example, constructing a catalogue that is usable by most library users and delivers relevant materials in the majority of cases is utilitarian. Library instruction that reaches most library users and can be assessed as improving the skills of most students is utilitarian. A modern catchphrase tells us not to let the perfect be the enemy of the good, and that, too, is a utilitarian approach. To many of us, however, such intense practicality leaves a void, a sense of longing for more meaning and richer philosophical underpinning.

In her subtle analysis of Andrew Osborn's pivotal article "The Crisis in Cataloging" (1941), H. M. Gallagher remarks that Dr. Osborn (himself trained as a philosopher) distinguished between "pragmatism" in its common meaning and the "American Pragmatism" of William James, John Dewey, and others.[2] The latter was concerned not just with "what works" but with the broader question of what it is we are trying to work toward or to achieve in the most efficient manner possible. She makes a very persuasive case that Osborn's article (which did change the face of cataloguing completely) was based on the attributes of American Pragmatism. This is significant, not least because the two strains of practicality and philosophy were united in Osborn's approach.[3]

If practical librarians do sustain a distrust of philosophy, the irony is that it will be in the face of the similarities between librarians and philosophers pointed out by philosophy professor Abraham Kaplan:

> Like your profession, mine also has thrust upon it, as its appropriate domain, the whole of knowledge, the whole of culture; nothing is supposed to be foreign to us, and we ought to be prepared under suitable circumstances to be helpful with regard to any and every area of human concern. Like you, we cannot even begin to occupy ourselves with the substance and content of this endless domain, but only with its form, with its structure, with its order, with the inter-relations of the various parts.[4]

Pragmatism and Idealism

Jesse Shera echoed Pierce Butler in stating, "librarians have seldom asked themselves about the philosophy of librarianship."[5] However, he went on to attempt a delineation of such a philosophy in the series of lectures from which that quotation comes. His idea of the profession of librarianship was of one rooted in two great ideas—service and a core of intellectual theory. The service rendered by librarians is performed, in Shera's words, "for the benefit of humanity and with a high sense of purpose and dedication."[6] That idea, expressed in that language, echoes a thought of Butler—"the librarian has come to conceive his office as a secular priesthood, administering a sacrament of cultural communion to individual souls."[7] This is high-flown but touches on the feeling that there is something intangible and important behind the work we do—a feeling that is at war with our predominant mode of practicality and prizing what works best. Archibald MacLeish, poet and Librarian of Congress, was of the same opinion and spoke of the "true library" asserting that "there is, indeed, a mystery of things" and, later in the same speech, of "the library's implicit assertion of the immanence of meaning."[8]

The conflict between pragmatism and idealism is inherent in our work, whether we think about it or not. Lee Finks, in a major but brief and accessible article, distinguishes between the need for library service and the urge that impels librarians to fulfill that need.[9] In his words, "It is . . . a noble urge, this altruism of ours, one that seems both morally and psychologically good." However, he also notes that libraries owe their existence to the fact that society needs us for practical reasons, and we must fulfill those practical needs or perish. Perhaps pragmatism and altruism/idealism are not in conflict but are two sides of the coin of what we do—complementary impulses and ways of thinking? Perhaps we should simply let our idealism inform our pragmatism while remembering that an impractical idealist is as much a menace to a library as is a practical librarian without visions and dreams.

To analyze the continuum of pragmatism to idealism in modern library philosophy, I will discuss the ideas on the topic of four twentieth-century librarians—S. R. Ranganathan, Jesse Shera, Samuel Rothstein, and Lee Finks.

Ranganathan's Five Laws

Shiyali Ramamrita Ranganathan (1892–1972) is, by common consent, the greatest figure of librarianship in the twentieth century. A mathematician by training, he brought to the study of library science (a term he invented) a belief in the scientific method and rational examination of social phenomena. Though best known for his considerable contributions to the theory of classification and subject retrieval, he studied all aspects of librarianship and, based on that study, formulated his famous *Five Laws of Library Science*. It would be more accurate to call them precepts rather than laws, but they are based on his scientific training, his training as a librarian (at University College, London), and his rigorous, objective analysis. The five laws are:

1. Books are for use.
2. Every book its reader.
3. Every reader his book.
4. Save the time of the reader.
5. The library is a growing organism.[10]

Though these laws are based on science and not philosophy, they do imply a context of values. If we examine them carefully, looking beyond the vocabulary of more than sixty years ago, we can see the values upon which they depend. The first law operates on a basis of *rationalism*. It tells us that collections are useful or they are nothing. Treating the word "books" as a surrogate for all library materials, we understand that all collection development policies (including decisions regarding which electronic resources are worth paying for) must be based on the application of reason. The rational approach is necessary if we are to answer the intensely practical question of which materials are useful to the members of the community that the library serves. The second and third laws are expressions of both *democracy* and *service*. It is democratic to say that all library users are entitled to the materials they need, and that materials should be selected with an eye to meeting those needs. Without the ethic of service in action, it would be difficult if not impossible for all library users to find the materials they need or for all materials to reach the users for whom they are intended. The fourth law is also rooted in *service* and is amazingly modern in that every modern work on service (in both the private and public sectors) stresses the importance of time saving. The fifth law is another product of *rationality*, but it is also related to *stewardship* in that libraries must allow for growth in their collections and services if they are to be good stewards for the indefinite future.

It is an audacious thing to propose laws that define a whole profession in just twenty-four words, but Ranganathan had an unshakable belief in his scientific approach. The fact that we can still find meaning across the decades in those twenty-four words is a justification of his audacity.

Shera's Social Epistemology

Jesse Hauck Shera came to call his redefinition of librarianship "social episte-mology" and discussed it in many of his writings.[11] *Epistemology* is defined as: "The study of the methods and the grounds of knowledge, esp. with reference to its limits and validity; broadly the theory of knowledge."[12] Shera's idea, there-fore, was to broaden librarianship to comprehend everything about the nature of knowledge and how it is recorded, preserved, transmitted, and so forth, in so-ciety. This is an expansive and scholarly view that goes beyond the narrow prag-matism that characterizes some library methods and policies, and, though Shera is famous as a "bookman," it transcends any particular medium by which knowledge is recorded and transmitted. He envisaged his epistemology—"a body of knowledge about knowledge itself"—as serving the individual but also as working toward our ultimate objective, the betterment of society.[13] He im-plies that betterment is the ultimate value that underlies all our work. The com-ponents of "social epistemology" as proposed by Shera are:

- the problem of how humans know
- the problem of how society knows and how the knowledge of an individ-ual becomes part of the knowledge possessed by society as a whole
- the history of knowledge and the philosophy of knowledge as it has evolved through time and across cultures
- existing library systems and how effective they are in meeting the com-munication needs of individuals and societies

This is not exactly a description of the curricula of today's successors to li-brary schools, but it would be hard to imagine a better basis for a would-be li-brarian's course of study.

Shera's concerns, in all his writings, are for knowledge, learning, scholar-ship, the transmission of the human record, and the role of the library in the improvement of society. He believed in the value of books and reading and, though not opposed to technology per se, was skeptical about the transforma-tional power of technology. In referring to the "information explosion" (a much-touted threat or promise of the 1960s), he quoted Archibald MacLeish with approval:

It is not additional "messages" we need, and least of all additional "messages" that merely tell us that the medium that communicates the message has changed the world. We *know* the world has changed. . . . What we do not know is how, precisely, it is changing and in what direction and with which consequences to ourselves.[14]

The values that we can derive by inference from Shera's social epistemology are *scholarship, stewardship, literacy and learning, service,* and *the good of society.*

Rothstein's Ethos

In 1967, Samuel Rothstein, the director of the library school at the University of British Columbia, gave a speech at the Canadian Library Association annual conference criticizing the ALA *Code of Ethics for Librarians* for its generality and banality.[15] He described that Code, in a magnificent phrase, as "fatuous adjurations"! His criticisms went beyond the deficiencies of that particular code of ethics to an attack on the very idea of a code of ethics having any relevance to work in libraries in the late 1960s. What we needed, in his opinion, was not such a code but a declaration of principles. The declaration would have three components:

- a statement of values, beliefs, and goals
- a description of the abilities and knowledge that are special to librarians
- a list of the dilemmas, problems, and issues that face librarians in particular

Rothstein's brief attempt to sketch such a statement of principles is of enduring interest, as is the linking of values, special abilities, and special issues that define librarianship. Rothstein listed four values:

- a special commitment to reading
- enlarging the horizons and elevating the taste of the community, using the discriminating selection of materials as a tool
- intellectual freedom
- helping people to secure the information they need

Have the passage of time and the burgeoning of technology rendered Rothstein's values outmoded? Before answering that question it is interesting to note his appraisal of the needs of library users more than thirty years ago and its similarity, rhetorically and substantially, to the common wisdom today. Before the personal computer, the Net and the Web, and cable television, before downsizing and job mobility, Rothstein wrote:

> In an age of mass media, which so often distort and debase communication, the library has a particularly important role to play in the fullest provision of impartial, many-sided information. In an age when information explodes and people must go on learning all their lives, librarians have a particularly important role to play in helping people secure the information they need.[16]

The world Rothstein saw seems to be different in degree rather than kind to the world we see today. Though couched in terms that are different from those with which we feel at ease today, his proposed values, I believe, still speak to us. Do we not believe that reading is "good and important" and that we should do all we can to foster it? The belief that reading lessens in importance because of technology is a common delusion of technophiles. The simple fact is that the ability to read and understand complex texts is central to the life of the mind. It is impossible to be educated and illiterate or aliterate at the same time. The first of Rothstein's values still stands.

It is possible that some will wince at the idea of librarians seeking to raise taste and encourage discrimination in the communities they serve. This is a noble goal but one that no longer has the foundation of belief that supported what was once a widely accepted view of the role of the librarian. It depends on the kind of library, I suppose. It is easier for a school librarian and a children's librarian to seek to raise the cultural level of students and children in general, but, even in that milieu, charges of elitism are easy to level. The ethos of the modern public library seems to be in direct conflict with the ideas of discriminating selection and elevating taste. Society no longer has a generally agreed definition of taste or culture and, even in the academy, "great books" programs are seen by many as a form of elitism. If Rothstein's second value survives at all today, it survives in individual acts of selection and recommendation—a kind of cultural guerrilla movement rather than a generally accepted belief in action.

Intellectual freedom is, broadly speaking, accepted as a key value of the profession of librarianship today as then. It is up against different challenges because of technology but the old challenges remain and the defense of intellectual freedom is no easier now than then. We should note that Rothstein's touchstone for the provision of library materials was legality. He wrote of the only acceptable censorship being that imposed by law and, even then, said that librarians should "hold themselves obliged to seek appropriate liberalizations in the law."[17] In most states and communities, laws concerned with intellectual freedom are more liberal now than they were thirty and more years ago, but the application of "community standards" in small communities provides a persistent threat to the intellectual freedom of those communities.

Rothstein's final value—helping people to secure the information they need—is surely unchallengeable today as it was then. When it comes down to it, libraries exist to make the connection between their users and the recorded knowledge and information they need and want. Everything that we do—building collections, installing gateways to electronic resources, performing reference work, providing bibliographic control, and on and on—is dedicated to that connection. The disputes are not about that value or the ends to which we are dedicated, but about how to realize them and which means should have higher priority than others.

It is interesting to note the abilities that Rothstein deemed necessary to realize his values and the problems and issues that stand in the way of that realization. (One can only admire the way in which he described the three parts of his statement of principles in what amounts to a one-page manifesto. Concision and clarity are not always found in library literature.) He thought a professional librarian should possess ability and skill in the following areas:

- collection development
- bibliographic control
- reference and information services
- reader's advisory work
- a specialized field, where appropriate
- administration

The issues and dilemmas he outlined also have a familiar ring:

> Is librarianship one profession or are we a loose confederation of related groups?
>
> "Do books and libraries and librarians have a future, or is librarianship as we know it to be phased out in favor of 'bits' and 'data banks' and documentalists?"[18]
>
> Are librarians educators or just technicians and managers?
>
> Do we try to reach everybody or just the small percentage that appreciates our services?
>
> Do librarians set policy or execute policy set by others?
>
> What is the relationship of the chief librarian to the professional staff—a first among equals or a general giving orders to subordinates?

It is not easy to believe that any of these questions has been answered satisfactorily or that any one of them, perhaps rephrased, has no resonance today. All go to the heart of the professional nature of librarianship—indeed, the very existence of that profession.

Rothstein believed that his delineation of our values, abilities, and dilemmas, considered together, constituted an "ethos"—the distinguishing characteristics that define librarians and librarianship. One might argue with some of the specifics but it is difficult to argue that his concept is irrelevant or his conclusions outdated.

Finks's Taxonomy of Values

Library educator Lee W. Finks is the author of the most important article on values in librarianship of the past few decades.[19] In it, he described his "personal taxonomy of values" divided into three broad categories accompanied by a category of "rival values." Finks' categories are:

- professional values
- general values
- personal values

Finks defined professional values as those that arise out of the nature of librarianship and the functioning of libraries in society. The first of these is *service*. As with the other values adduced by Finks that are the subject of a chapter in the present book, I will not dwell on this value here but use Finks' description in the appropriate chapter. His second professional value is *stewardship*. By this he means not only our responsibility for passing the records of humanity intact to future generations, but also our duty to be good stewards in our everyday work. We must ensure that we are seen to be, in his words, "honest, industrious men and women who know our jobs and do them well." His next subcategory of professional values is itself a group that he calls *philosophical values*. They are a belief in reason and learning, a respect for scholarship, neutrality in the "battle of competing ideas," and prizing the good over the trivial and vulgar. Then come *democratic values*—an attachment to democracy as a societal ideal and openness to all kinds and conditions of people. His last professional value is an attachment to *reading and books*. Even eleven years ago, his blunt statement that "we are bookish" may have been less debatable than it is now. One would like to hope that most librarians are indeed women and men who love books and reading and find the latter "a superior way to pass the time," but it may not be so. It is certainly a value that I share and one that is essential to the survival of libraries, but it is not something that all librarians *must* adhere to in order to do their work. In my sunset years, I would guess that this is an issue that breaks largely on generational grounds. I suspect, without empirical proof, that a reverence for books and reading is all but universal in librarians over the age of fifty and less commonly found in those below middle age.

Finks defines general values as those that are shared by "normal, healthy people, whatever their field." (One of the many engaging things about this seminal article is the robust directness of Finks' views and worldview.) He calls the first group of general values *work values*. This term encompasses competence, professional autonomy, and the search for excellence. He quite correctly points out that the realization of these values depends greatly on the environment within which the individual librarian works. It should be sobering for all library administrators to realize that even the most gifted and dedicated librarians cannot reach their goals and fulfill their aspirations unless the library in which they work has an atmosphere and actuality that allows the fullest flowering of abilities and ideals. Values only work in places in which they are allowed and encouraged to work. Finks' next grouping is *social values*. These include tolerance and respect for others and all the other things that we are supposed to learn in kindergarten and carry throughout our lives. The reader realizes that she is reading someone from the idealistic end of the pragmatism–idealism scale when Finks mentions optimism and comes up with the sentence that summarizes what all his values are about—"Being happy librarians in happy libraries; it is not an impossible dream." His last general values group is *satisfaction values*. These might be summed up as the fact that it is impossible for us to serve individuals and society unless we have self-respect and self-esteem.

Finks' personal values are those that apply particularly to librarians as a class. Without falling into stereotyping or rejecting the diversity of our profession, it is possible to agree with Finks that most librarians share or aspire to certain characteristics. He defines them as *humanistic values, idealistic values, conservative values,* and *aesthetic values.* I share Finks' view that most librarians are humanists and idealists believing, in his words, "that the human spirit can flourish" and hoping for "inspiration, self-realization, and the growth of wisdom in all people." I also agree that most librarians are (very small "c") conservative in that we tend to prefer steady evolutionary change, order over disorder, and standardization. (Many years ago, I was told that hard-core cataloguers always vote for the party in power because, if it wins, there will be far fewer government headings to change in the catalogue!) Finks points out that our innate conservatism is a necessary curb on our idealism—the yin and yang of a librarian's soul. Last, I agree that aesthetics are important to librarians. We seek to satisfy our aesthetic sense through harmony in the architecture of library buildings, beauty in literature, music, and the arts, and even elegance in library systems.

This idealistic and optimistic picture of librarians and their values is constantly threatened, in Finks' view, by what he calls rival values—*bureaucracy, anti-intellectualism,* and *nihilism.* Bureaucracy can sometimes be found in small libraries and is endemic in large libraries. It is, in one sense, the natural product of our desire for order and regular procedure. There is an anti-intellectual tinge to much of the discourse about technology that can be found in statements that equate the Internet and a research library or Web surfing and serious reading. We stand for excellence and the intellect, for scholarship and culture or we stand for nothing. Nihilism is the philosophy of the despairing, and a librarian who loses faith in the future of libraries or the value of librarianship is succumbing to that despair.

Finks' values and taxonomy of values are the most important accessible statements on the topic in many years. If every librarian were to absorb them into her or his working life, the future of libraries would be both guaranteed and bright.

Central or "Core" Values

My reading and distillation of the four authors discussed here and other writings on librarianship have led me to formulate the following eight central values of librarianship. I am sure that the list of values that I offer is different from those that others might advance, but it is difficult to believe that these values (possibly with different wording) would not show up on any composite list.

Stewardship

> preserving the human record to ensure that future generations know what we know

> caring for and nurturing of education for librarianship so that we pass on our best professional values and practices

> being good stewards of our libraries so that we earn the respect of our communities

Service

> ensuring that all our policies and procedures are animated by the ethic of service to individuals, communities, society, and posterity

> evaluating all our policies and procedures using service as a criterion

Intellectual freedom

> maintaining a commitment to the idea that all people in a free society should be able to read and see whatever they wish to read and see
>
> defending the intellectual freedom of all members of our communities
>
> defending the free expression of minority opinion
>
> making the library's facilities and programs accessible to all

Rationalism

> organizing and managing library services in a rational manner
>
> applying rationalism and the scientific method to all library procedures and programs

Literacy and learning

> encouraging literacy and the love of learning
>
> encouraging lifelong sustained reading
>
> making the library a focus of literacy teaching

Equity of access to recorded knowledge and information

> ensuring that all library resources and programs are accessible to all
>
> overcoming technological and monetary barriers to access

Privacy

> ensuring the confidentiality of records of library use
>
> overcoming technological invasions of library use

Democracy

> playing our part in maintaining the values of a democratic society
>
> participating in the educational process to ensure the educated citizenry that is vital to democracy
>
> employing democracy in library management

I examine each of these values in a chapter in this book with an eye to describing the present state of libraries and the likely future of libraries and librarianship.

Having listed the core values of librarianship, let us consider the value of libraries . . .

NOTES

1. Pierce Butler, *An Introduction to Library Science* (Chicago: University of Chicago Pr., 1993; Phoenix Books, 1961), xi.

2. H. M. Gallagher, "Dr. Osborn's 1941 'The Crisis in Cataloging': A Shift in Thought toward American Pragmatism," *Cataloging and Classification Quarterly* 12, nos. 3/4 (1991): 3–33.

3. For a further discussion of "The Crisis in Cataloging," see Michael Gorman, "1941: An Analysis and Appreciation of Andrew Osborn's 'The Crisis in Cataloging,'" *Serials Librarian* 6, nos. 2–3 (winter 1981/spring 1982), 127–131.

4. Abraham Kaplan, "The Age of the Symbol," in *The Intellectual Foundations of Library Education,* ed. Don R. Swanson (Chicago: University of Chicago Pr., 1965), 7–16.

5. J. H. Shera, *Sociological Foundations of Librarianship* (Bombay: Asia Publishing House, 1970), 29.

6. Ibid.

7. Butler, *An Introduction to Library Science,* xiii.

8. Archibald MacLeish, "The Premise of Meaning," *American Scholar* 41 (summer 1972): 357–362, adapted from an address delivered at the opening of the library of York University, Toronto.

9. Lee W. Finks, "Values without Shame," *American Libraries* (April 1989): 352–356.

10. S. R. Ranganathan, *The Five Laws of Library Science,* 2d ed. (Bombay; reprint, New York: Asia Publishing House, 1963).

11. See, for example, Jesse H. Shera, "Toward a Theory of Librarianship and Information Science," in his *Knowing Books and Men: Knowing Computers Too* (Littleton, Colo.: Libraries Unlimited, 1973), 93–110.

12. *Webster's New International Dictionary,* 3d ed.

13. Shera, "Toward a Theory of Librarianship," 95–96.

14. Archibald MacLeish, *Champion of a Cause* (Chicago: ALA, 1971), 246.

15. Samuel Rothstein, "In Search of Ourselves," *Library Journal* (January 15, 1968): 156–157; see also the *Code of Ethics,* promulgated in 1938 and reprinted in the *American Library Annual, 1958* (New York: Bowker, 1958), 111–112.

16. Rothstein, "In Search of Ourselves."

17. Ibid.

18. Ibid.

19. Finks, "Values without Shame."

2

The Value
of Libraries

When the Good Times Ended

The idea of the public library is, on the face of it, an improbable one. Only recently in human history has there been widespread agreement that people have human rights deserving of universal respect. (Remember that the United States enforced chattel slavery until 1865.) The idea that every person should be educated is an even more recent and radical one. And the idea that society should provide its members with the means to continue their education independently was more radical still.[1]

The radical notion in the last sentence of this quotation encapsulates the true value of libraries: Libraries allow every person in the community served to continue her or his education, to become more knowledgeable, and to live the life of the mind in the way in which she or he chooses. This essence of the value of all libraries is sometimes obscured by the day-to-day minutiae of library use. A person asking a question in a corporate library, a child listening to a story in a children's library, a person consulting an academic library's online catalogue—none of these may be thinking of himself or herself as being engaged in lifelong learning, but each of them is.

What is the value of libraries? Through lifelong learning, libraries can and do change lives, a point that cannot be overstated. Within that overarching value, and depending on the community it serves, a library is one or more of the following:

- a focal point of a community
- the heart of the university
- the one good place in a city
- the collective memory of a research institution
- the place remembered fondly by children when grown
- the solace of the lonely and the lost
- the place in which all are welcome
- a source of power through knowledge

When you look at libraries over the years, it is easy to see that the public perception has varied and, though libraries are almost always viewed positively, they are not always understood and prized for what they are. The phase we are going through now illustrates that well. Public misunderstanding of technology and its potential has led to misunderstanding of the reality of libraries and of their present state and possible futures. So, let us look at the development of libraries and at the threats and alternatives with which we are faced.

Libraries over the Years

An unprecedented growth in libraries and development of the profession of librarianship took place in the United States, the United Kingdom, and Canada from the latter half of the nineteenth century to the end of the 1920s. Thousands of libraries of all kinds were built (many with the conscience money of Andrew Carnegie). The great public and private university libraries of the United States came to flower. Public library service was extended to almost every citizen. The profession of librarianship saw the establishment of national library associations; the creation of a system of library education; the beginning of scientific study of libraries and their users; and the intellectual innovations of cataloguing codes, classification schemes, professional journals, and collaborative systems of all kinds. In less than a century, modern libraries and librarianship were born and came to maturity and self-confidence. It was an age of great achievements and of heroes and heroines—the first but not the last Golden Age of Libraries. The interwar years of prosperity and depression followed those years of the founding of the modern library. Libraries grew in number and size in the 1920s and were an incalculable public good in the hard years of the 1930s. Libraries survived the Second World War, as did many social entities, with a feeling that, with fascism defeated, we were in for progress as far as the eye could see.

In those years following the last Good War, many librarians assumed that libraries were so patently, palpably good that they needed no justification. They had a basis for that opinion. Communities took their libraries for granted; academic institutions competed with each other about their libraries and boasted of the size of the collections and the excellence of their staff; schools gave pride of place to their libraries and librarians; and companies, governments, and other entities developed libraries and library services at a great pace. This largely happy state of affairs came to a screeching halt sometime between the first Carter energy crisis in the 1970s and the first Reagan recession in the 1980s. Decline and decay became the order of the day, and most libraries hit rock bottom in the early 1990s. Funding (or rather the lack of it) was the main proximate cause of this fall from grace. It would be a grave mistake to blame funding alone. The fact is that the precipitous decline in funding occurred at almost the same time as the steep increase in the cost of library materials (especially serials) and the rise in electronic technology as an additional and much-desired cost center. The combination of these factors was almost a deathblow for some and a grievous problem for all. In the early days of the automation of library processes, many administrators (and even some librarians who should have known better) really believed that it would save money. Similarly, the extraordinarily rapid growth in the number of electronic resources available to libraries and their users caused some to believe that those resources would supplant expensive collections and services. In both cases, the opposite has proven to be true. Automated library processes are more cost-efficient than manual processes, but that is because they increase efficiency, not because they lower costs. Equally, apart from the signal examples of indexing and abstracting services, electronic resources have replaced almost no "traditional" resources and services and have proven to be just another consumer of the library budget pie. When electronic resources are valuable, they are, in most instances, enhancements, not replacements, of other collections and services.

Going Virtual?

Before we discuss alternatives to the "traditional" library, it would be well to describe that library. I use the word "traditional" with great reluctance and simply for want of anything better—its pejorative overtones of clinging to the past, of being place-centered and exclusively book-centered, bear no relationship to the experience of modern libraries. The only other available term—"real library"—implies that there is something illusory about the term "virtual library." Though tempting at times, it is a serious mistake to treat the virtual library as merely high-tech smoke and mirrors, though most writings in favor of virtual libraries have a decidedly glassy and cloudy aspect smacking more of conjuration than reality.

The "Traditional" Library

Formulated by understanding and analysis of the traditions and history of libraries, my idea of a "traditional" library is of one that selects, collects, and gives access to all the forms of recorded knowledge and information that are relevant to its mission and to the needs of the community it serves, and assists and instructs in the use of those resources. More than that, the "traditional" library welcomes, as it always has, new forms of communicating knowledge and information—including electronic resources.[2] The "traditional" library is not one that rejects change and innovation—it is a library that welcomes all means of serving its community better. The conflict between "traditional" libraries and "virtual" libraries turns out, under examination, to be an elaborate kabuki dance choreographed carefully by those who think that real libraries are obsolescent. The true choice is between real libraries with a substantial component of electronic services and collections, on the one hand, and a replacement that has *only* electronic services and collections, on the other. There are those who seriously believe that the second prediction of the future will actually come about. They are not all wild-eyed technophiles prophesying the imminent "death of the book," even though they do believe that, sometime in the lifetime of most of us, electronic communication will be the only medium.[3] Some digital true believers are among the best-known names in our profession. Frederick Kilgour, the founder and sole begetter of OCLC—the most successful cooperative venture in the history of librarianship—wrote this in 1983:

> The electronic files of documents currently coming into existence will *soon* [my emphasis] be the logical equivalent, and replacement of [*sic*], collections of publications in classical libraries, and libraries as we know them will diminish in usefulness.[4]

Librarian and writer about libraries Charles Martell argues that "physical existence is *not* [my emphasis] a necessary criterion for the library of the future."[5] He cites the many similarities between libraries and computers—the ability to store "vast amounts of information," convenient location, and so on—and argues that the only unique function of the library is the provision of study space. He illustrates this uniquely reductionist view with the example of his personal library of photography books, which he has replaced by access to the same images on the Internet and a "little color printer." This illustration is, to put it mildly, intellectually unsatisfying in that it argues a generality from a small specialized example, and, furthermore, one that depends on images, not texts. Few would argue that the Internet is inefficient at delivering such images as can be located to anyone with a little color printer. Even using that example, is it really true that all the images in Martell's small photography library are available on the Internet? Is the image produced by his little color printer even remotely comparable to high-quality print on paper? Even if the answers to these questions were positive (which, if I were a gambler, I would bet is not the case), what does that tell us about a vast repository of recorded knowledge and information organized for ready access (the library) as compared to the strikingly disorganized Internet and Web? Precious little, I fear. Proponents of the virtual library will, of course, say that we are on the low beginners' slope of the mighty mountain yet to be born, but one cannot analyze predictions, promises, and virtual sleight of hand—still less refute them.

The "Virtual" Library

The alternative to real libraries is sometimes called "the library without walls"—a silly term that implies current library service is contained entirely within the walls of library buildings. It is sometimes called "the digital library" and, other times, "the virtual library." In a remarkable paper, Jean-Claude Guédon demonstrates that the two latter terms are not synonymous.[6] "Digital" refers to the practice of recording information in terms of zeros and ones—that is, a means of recording and storing that is different in kind but not in degree from other means. One might as well refer to a nineteenth-century library as a "letters-on-paper library." In Guédon's thinking, the term "virtual library" refers to something a good deal more ambitious—one in which all the library's functions, processes, staffing, mission, and purpose are reconsidered, reorganized, and shaped around digital documents. Whether such a transformation is practical, possible, or even desirable is the central question of the future of libraries. There are, when it comes down to it, only the two mutually exclusive alternatives. One, which has the weight of history behind it, is the library of the past and today incorporating electronic resources into its programs, collections, and services, and making the necessary changes to allow that incorporation. This is what libraries have done over the centuries as new means of communication (printed texts, printed music, cartographic materials, sound recordings, films of all kinds) have arisen and, because of that process, libraries have been changed and enriched while preserving a tradition that spanned the centuries. The alternative—the virtual library—calls for a break with that tradition—the complete replacement of all other forms of communication in favor of digital documents. We should note that the balance of "traditional" resources and services will vary greatly from library to library, depending on the type of library and the clientele served. The range will have medical, law, and science and technical (for example, engineering) libraries (with a preponderant reliance on electronic resources and services) at one end, and rare book and children's libraries at the other. The latter will have an electronic component but the proportion will be much smaller.

The virtual library calls for the demolition of the traditional library (literally as well as figuratively) and new ways of looking at every aspect of the library. In fact, there is good reason to ask if the word "library" is applicable in any sense when talking about the "virtual library." Guédon is at pains to point out that there is a difference between "virtual" and "unreal" in this context, stating that "the virtual is nothing but potential and as such it is reality (possibly) in the making."[7] Martell echoes Guédon in saying, "The creation of a readily identifiable 'intellectual and logical' cyberspace for libraries will be of the utmost importance . . . decades from now when the physical library will be less visible to the public than the virtual library in the new cyberspace environment."[8]

These are fascinating, if complicated, topics, and Guédon's and Martell's vision of the virtual library as a transformation in the act of becoming is a welcome change from the dreary mechanism and determinism of most writers on the topic. However, no matter if one approaches the virtual library as a vision or as a technical process, there are some unavoidable questions to be asked and some hard answers to be sought. The first question, and the hardest to answer, is why.

Why the Virtual Library?

It seems that proponents of the virtual library have only three possible answers to that short question. The first is practical—the ease of access from a computer and the increase in access for people distant from physical libraries are seen as outweighing any and all of the disadvantages of digital documents (for example, being mutable, perishable, and unverifiable). The second is teleological—that there is a grand design and the virtual library represents an inevitable manifestation of progress toward the fulfillment of that design. To believers, there is an inevitability about each innovation in human communication, and each innovation is demonstrably superior to its predecessors.[9] The only other answer is "why not?"—one that is offered implicitly by those who take up each fad and accept without question banal phrases like "the Age of Information." I discuss rationalism and irrationalism elsewhere in this book, but pause here to suggest that answers to "why the virtual library?" that are based on belief in a grand design or on unthinking acceptance are not intellectually coherent. The practical arguments are more easily quantified and can be used to justify a virtual component of library service but, by no means, the idea of a totally virtual library. Moreover, even if you believe that electronic communication is part of a great plan, it is difficult to argue that each form of communicating and recording knowledge is superior to its predecessors. What happens is that human beings concentrate on the positive aspects of all innovations and tend to underplay or stay willfully ignorant of the negative consequences and attributes until they are so manifest—often long after the bloom is off the rose—that they can no longer be ignored. Proponents of electronic communication stress the ease and speed with which messages are created and disseminated, but rarely dwell on their lack of durability. Politicians and computer scientists press for schools to be wired to give all schoolchildren access to the Net and the Web, but ignore the underfunded libraries in those same schools and the negative effect of such neglect on reading and the literacy levels of those schoolchildren. Futurists predict that electronic technology will supplant "the book" sooner rather than later, but ignore the fact that technology has made book production and high production values quicker, easier, cheaper, and more accessible to more publishers.

Beyond these examples lies the Law of Unintended Consequences. The postwar history of California is the classic instance of that law. Did those who boosted the development of southern California really intend to destroy an agrarian way of life, pollute the air and water, create a strip mall automotive culture, and go far to injure the very characteristics that led millions to move to the Golden State? Similarly, will the ease of electronic communication blind its advocates to the possibilities of the loss of substantial parts of the human record in an age of virtual libraries, and the creation of a world that has abandoned learning and is pervaded by isolation and anomie?

Living with Virtual Libraries

What would the world be like if all libraries as we know them now were to be replaced by virtual libraries? Let us go to, say, March 6, 2011—as good a date as any because those who believe in the virtual library are necessarily vague as to when it will reach fruition—and assume that virtual libraries have taken over. We find a world in which the following things have happened:

1. The buildings we now call libraries have been demolished or turned into indoor markets, skating rinks, cyber cafes, homeless shelters, or any of the other purposes to which they could be adapted.

2. Recorded sound, movies, videos, multimedia creations, and so on are available from your home or office computer, which has been transmogrified into a total all-singing, all-dancing communication center.

3. You have replaced your telephones, personal computers, televisions, CD players, VCRs, home entertainment centers, stereos, and all the other gadgets that we use for edification and relaxation with that communication center.

4. Most of the books and other printed items in research libraries have been transferred to huge warehouses (one copy of each title only) scattered across the nation or have been discarded.

5. The stocks of other libraries have been pulped or burned or given to third world countries.

6. Attempts to digitize a respectable percentage of the recorded knowledge and information found in print have run into copyright, technical, and funding problems that have proven to be insurmountable.

7. Most publishers of books and magazines have gone out of business. Those that remain publish small runs of hand-printed items for a small population of hobbyist readers; large runs of trashy magazines, pornography, and comic books for a dwindling, aging readership; or samizdat books for cultural guerrillas.

8. Scholarly journals have been replaced by a clearinghouse system for articles run by a consortium of universities. The rise of commercial "virtual universities" and the end of the tenure system in real universities mean that fewer articles are handled by the clearinghouse each year but there is a greater traffic between (mostly elderly) scholars in invisible colleges.

9. Because the problems of producing an "e-book" that is "just as good as a book" have proven to be insuperable and because few people engage in sustained reading of long, complex texts, the vast majority of functionally literate people content themselves with reading brief texts from screens or from printouts.

10. The vast majority of young people are functionally literate, if they can read at all, and easy prey to the commercial, political, and societal manipulation that emanates from their multimedia entertainment centers.

These predictions may seem unduly pessimistic. They are, however, merely the logical extensions of some of the facts and trends we see today projected into an all-digital future, and of the economic and social consequences of a massive move from a print culture to an electronic culture.

What Happens to the Books?

Public and school libraries would cease to exist. In poor communities, they would be replaced by communal communications centers with batteries of terminals connected to the Net, the Web, and their successors. University libraries as we know them would cease to exist. The world of academia is one in which most students and faculty interact only with electronic resources and with each other at a distance. Almost all teaching and learning have been reduced to distant learning using television and the Web. The collections of all these libraries will have to be disposed of, because they will not be used. The sight of universities and colleges ridding themselves of collections that took hundreds of millions of dollars to build might be distressing at first, but would become commonplace and easily ignored. Keeping even one copy of each title in a warehouse would be quite expensive, and the future of those warehouses would be problematic as the habit of sustained reading gradually died. Digitizing even a small proportion of the knowledge and information contained in those books would be an enormously expensive enterprise. It is likely that the majority of books would not be included in even the most ambitious digitizing projects and, thus, a major part of the human record would be lost to posterity. If you think this is an extreme prediction, just consider that the university librarian of a major research library is in the habit of referring to that library's books as "legacy collections." If a chilling phrase like that comes readily to the lips of a librarian, imagine how little others of power and influence think of book collections and how readily they will dispose of them.

Electronic Journals

The future of scholarly communication in the form of articles is even cloudier than that of other library materials. The great majority of electronic journals, newspapers, and so forth that exist today are by-products of the print publishing industry. They are available to us, and only available to us, because the companies and institutions that produce them make money by selling the print issues. There is a tiny minority of truly electronic journals and magazines, most of which are subsidized by not-for-profit bodies or run at a loss. It is hard to envision an economic model that would support a profitable electronic journal publishing industry. In this context, the story of *Slate*—the online magazine subsidized by Bill Gates—is instructive. *Slate* is issued over the Internet and is available to all without payment. The plan was to move to a subscription basis after establishing the magazine. When that move was made, and despite the excellence and star power of its journalists, the subscription model failed. Too few people subscribed and those people could not be prevented from disseminating their paid copy to others without further payment. *Slate* still exists, is still available free, and still loses money. Because its angel is the richest man in the world, it will probably continue to exist indefinitely, but it scarcely constitutes a viable model for the rest of us.

The journal as a form of scholarly communication was born in eighteenth-century Britain as a means of disseminating interesting findings in many fields (natural history, philosophy, etc.) among a small group of wealthy polymaths. Its evolution into today's massive apparatus of microspecializations is wearisomely familiar, as is the burden that apparatus has imposed on academic libraries. Many librarians are salivating at the prospect of seeing the back of the scholarly journal, but they may be rejoicing too soon. If the print journal were to die, there is no evidence whatever that it would be replaced by some orderly, economically feasible system of electronic dissemination. I think it is quite plausible that the twenty-first century will see something like the eighteenth century, only viewed through a glass darkly. Economics are paramount, but possible changes in academia may have just as great an effect. If the print journal industry collapsed, most of today's electronic journals would vanish (because they are by-products, not autonomous publications). The rise of proprietary "universities" and the death of the tenure system will probably cause the number of potential articles to decline by more than 90 percent. What would remain? To begin with, remaining scholars in the "poor" disciplines will form electronically linked "invisible colleges," in which they will exchange articles, much as eighteenth-century scholars wrote for journals and exchanged lengthy learned letters with their peers. There might be some money to be made in the "rich" disciplines, in which case the monied scientific, medical, and technical communities will evolve a new type of exchange of research results based on fees and purchase. If you think that academia is isolated from society now, just wait until the time when a few scholars in the liberal arts and sciences communicate only with each other, and scientists, technologists, and medical people sell their research results to mega-companies in a system in which the sole and ultimate value is profit.

What Happens to Reading?

The world of the virtual library is a world of graphics, short texts, videos, and sound recordings. Anyone whose intellectual life is predicated on interaction with a personal communication center will soon lose the habit of reading, because true literacy (as opposed to functional literacy) will be an unnecessary skill. The search for the e-book that is a satisfactory replacement for real books will not be successful, but that will not matter because sustained reading will be a habit of a dwindling few and, eventually, a lost art. Is there anyone who thinks that the world will be better off when reading is infrequent and devoted only to short bites of "information"?

What Happens to Librarians?

I suppose a few librarians might be gainfully employed in a world of virtual libraries. It is difficult to see much more than that. After all, most of our skills and abilities either will not apply or will not be valued. When the libraries are closed and all their former users are at home interacting with their total communication installation and settling for anything that a search engine can find for them, what could a librarian do to help? It is not just that our unique skills—bibliographic control, collection development, reference work, and so on—would not apply. It is not even that our values—service, intellectual freedom, and the like—would not apply. It is that the great enterprises of learning, human progress, and the betterment of society would be irrelevant in a world of images and thought bites, a world in which human society regresses to the point at which it consists of isolated individuals living bemused, intellectually stunted lives in electronic Lascaux caves.

The One Good Thing . . .

. . . is that *it will not happen!* It will not happen because humanity is, in the end, both practical and idealistic. We will keep and cherish all the forms of communication (including the book) that we have now because they are useful and because they work. Learning and scholarship and libraries will continue because human beings love them for their own sakes and because they make life and society better. We will continue to incorporate electronic technology into our libraries and lives for practical reasons and because, rightly used, that technology can enhance real libraries and bring illumination and pleasure to individual lives and to society.

Why Libraries Will Survive

I believe libraries are valued by many different and influential sectors of society. That esteem and positive valuation may be more latent than overt, but it is there and we need to capitalize on it. One of the most malignant of the many poor public policy frameworks in California is the necessity for fund-raising proposals to achieve a two-thirds majority of those voting. This means that it is very hard to raise money for even the most worthwhile government expenditures—the not-so-secret aim of those who created this obstacle. The positive result of this generally negative situation is that it has forced those seeking to increase funding for public services (including librarians and friends of libraries) to work to bring out their vote. In the process, libraries routinely garner handsome majorities for their bonds, even when the proposal fails because the "yes" vote is less than 66.67 percent. This is an object lesson for all of us: The votes and the people who value libraries are there—they just need to be informed, courted, and energized. The time has gone, if it ever was, when we could be confident that our libraries and their funding would be supported without question. The lesson is that we all have to work in formal and informal ways to increase and maintain support for libraries among as many people and groups as we can. We certainly should not shrink from modern persuasive techniques—advertising, public relations, and so on—or from locating and tapping alternative sources of funding. The truth about "traditional" and "virtual" libraries is one of the vital things that we should explain to the wider world. We have a lot to combat. For example, it is astonishing to me that many educated people still swallow the virtual hype and, without any malice toward libraries and learning, assume that "the book" is dying or already dead.

We should begin with our natural supporters—older people, parents, teachers and faculty, scholars and researchers, education- and literacy-minded politicians (not all of whom are progressive in other areas of public policy), and general users of libraries. Securing your base is a political axiom but so is the idea that you cannot win with only the base on your side. That means that libraries, individually and collectively, need to identify other groups that might not be thought of as library supporters, especially those with money and influence. Though we may wish it were not, library funding is a political issue and one that needs to be addressed as such. That includes the dissemination and clarification of the positive image of the library and the countering and obliteration of any negative images. For example, how many people on a university campus realize that, 99 percent of the time, the library is the, or one of the, most technologically advanced units in the academy? Have people who still see libraries as hushed, repressive places even been in a children's or college library lately? Do most people realize the depth and breadth of the collections held by major city public libraries?

There has been a lot of discussion and writing about the importance of "advocacy" of libraries.[10] Used in this specialized manner, "advocacy" means organized, continuing discussion of the value of libraries (particularly as a source of access to electronic resources) and pressure on politicians to maintain and increase library funding. My belief is that this advocacy is best done by individuals and by local and regional library groupings, rather than by national associations of librarians. However it is done, libraries have a compelling story and librarians have a duty to tell that story. This is particularly true in this time, in which the implicitly antilibrary exaggerations of technophiles too often go unanswered. We should not shrink from using all possible means of communication and all possible political strategies to tell our story and assert our value.

The public's perception of the value of libraries is tied, to a great extent, to their perception of the library as place . . .

NOTES

1. Fred Lerner, *The Story of Libraries* (New York: Continuum, 1998), 138.

2. See the idea of the "electronic library" in Michael Buckland, *Redesigning Library Services: A Manifesto* (Chicago: ALA, 1992).

3. See, for example, Andrew Odlyzko, "Silicon Dreams and Silicon Bricks," *Library Trends* 46, no. 1 (summer 1997): 152–167.

4. Frederick Kilgour, "The Online Catalog Revolution," in *New Trends in Electronic Publishing and Electronic Libraries* (Essen [Germany]: Essen University Library, 1984).

5. Charles Martell, "Going, Going, Gone," *Journal of Academic Librarianship* 25, no. 3 (May 1999): 224–225.

6. Jean-Claude Guédon, *The Virtual Library: An Oxymoron?* (The 1998 Joseph Leiter lecture). *http://www.mlanet.org/publications/bmla/leiter98.html*

7. Ibid.

8. Martell, "Going, Going, Gone."

9. See, for example, Frederick Kilgour, *The Evolution of the Book* (New York: Oxford University Pr., 1998).

10. See, for example, Patricia Glass Schuman, "Speaking Up and Speaking Out," *American Libraries* 30, no. 9 (October 1999): 50–53.

3

The Library
as Place

There was a time when the idea of the library (an abstraction made up of all library collections, staff, services, and programs) and the place called the library were coterminous. As technology has enabled some library services to be available away from the place called the library, it has made that place less important in some people's minds. The whole idea of the virtual library is an implicit challenge to the idea of the library as place and must be measured in that light. The notion is seductive on its face—all the citizens of a digital nation finding all they need in the way of recorded knowledge and information without having to leave their homes. Such an idea depends, essentially, on three things:

- that all recorded knowledge and information be available, and permanently available, in digital form;
- that all recorded knowledge and information be organized and readily retrievable; and
- that all individuals be able to interact fruitfully with the universe of recorded knowledge and information without the assistance of any other humans.

It is almost impossible to overestimate how far we are from those three basic requirements. Let us take the recorded knowledge and information that is the traditional concern of libraries (as opposed to the oceans of disorganized information found on the Net—the kind of thing that the Research Libraries Group's Walt Crawford calls "stuff"). By this, I mean the organized, edited, filtered, and formally published recorded knowledge and information created over the centuries and found in books, printed serials, cartographic materials, and so on. For monographic items, the amount available in digital form is certainly less than 5 percent. Most *current* scholarly journals and other periodicals are available in digital form and the efforts of JSTOR and other initiatives are pushing that availability back a few years for, as yet, a relatively small number of serials. Even so, the digital availability of serial recorded knowledge and information is probably less than 10 percent of the total produced now and in the past (higher for scholarly serials than for popular serial publications). It is well worth noting here that the availability of current journals in digital form is, with very few exceptions, a by-product of the print journals from which their publishers make money. There is, at this time, no economic model of digital-only journal publishing that makes sense. We can see this both in the numbers of such publications and in their origins. The tiny number of digital-only journals is less significant than the fact that those that do exist are either the product of the not-for-profit sector (universities, learned associations, etc.) or ego-driven loss leaders like *Slate*.

The "stuff" that the Net has added to "traditional" recorded knowledge and information is unorganized and largely unretrievable according to the most minimal library standards. I know of no one who believes that anything but a small fraction of the world's recorded knowledge and information now available in print will ever be digitized (for a variety of financial, technical, and copyright reasons). I know of no one who believes that the authority control and controlled vocabularies that are essential for good retrieval will ever be applied comprehensively to the swamp of digital "stuff." Then there is the question of unmediated interaction with digital documents. If you doubt that there is a great need for assistance in the use of digital documents, just ask any modern reference librarian.

All this adds up to the incontrovertible fact that we need physical libraries—places called libraries—for the indefinite future for the following purposes:

- to house the print and other tangible collections—not only those from the past but also those that will be created in the future
- to house spaces for people to study, to do research, and to read, view, and listen for pleasure
- to provide places in which any person (including the poor and otherwise disadvantaged) can obtain access to the Net, the Web, and the whole range of electronic resources, and can obtain assistance in their use

- to provide areas for specialized collections and associated library services (sound recording and video libraries, rare book rooms, manuscript collections and archives, etc.)
- to provide meeting places within the community served by the library
- to provide suitable spaces in which library users can be assisted by professionals
- to provide suitable spaces for instruction (library instruction, literacy teaching, information competence) leading to the empowerment of members of the library community

The Human Dimension

We also need the library as a place because we are human beings. "The library" (the building that houses both the physical library and its immanence) is always one of the focal points of its community. From the great national libraries to rooms called "the library" in high schools and corporations, there is tremendous force in the library idea made manifest in buildings and public spaces.

Let us consider another kind of public place. Religious people may, and do, pray in private, but most feel the need to assemble in churches, temples, synagogues, mosques, and other places dedicated to the idea of religion. Why do they do that? Certainly it is to get the assistance and mediation of people—priests, imams, rabbis, bonzes—more learned in their religion than they. Equally surely, it is because of the human need to gather with other humans and, in so doing, to sanctify that place of assembly so that even, say, a revival tent becomes a sacred place. It can scarcely be considered too far-fetched to suggest that there is a parallel with libraries. They are places that embody learning, culture, and other important secular values and manifestations of the common good, and there is a need arising from our common humanity to visit such places. People go to them for the assistance to be obtained from other people—librarians in this case—who are more knowledgeable than they about recorded knowledge and information. Also, just as individuals go to religious buildings to pray alone sometimes, individuals go to libraries sometimes to pursue their interests without assistance from librarians. Analogies are treacherous things, more often misleading than illuminating, but I think it is worth at least a passing thought that TV evangelism and religious sites on the Net have not led to calls to replace religious buildings with "virtual houses of worship." Come to think, shopping by catalogue, on television, and on the Net have not led to calls for "virtual shopping malls." There is a human need for human contact and appropriate buildings in which to gather, and the believers in "virtual libraries" ignore that need at their peril.

What is the alternative to the bleak vision of the virtual library advocates? I believe the answer lies in exactly the opposite direction—in expanding the roles of the library as place, not in abolishing that public place. Robert Mc-Nulty says:

> A library can be "the great good place in the city"—a literacy, Internet, and film center, a place for lectures, concerts, and exhibitions. . . . A library can also host coffee houses and restaurants, serve as an information center for visiting tourists, be a safe place for kids and a meeting spot for civic groups.[1]

(Neal Pierce points out that Andrew Carnegie built a boxing gymnasium into one of his Pittsburgh libraries and a swimming pool into another, so the idea of the expansive library as place is hardly new.[2]) A friend who runs a small public library in Iowa gave me the following list of activities in, and functions of, her library:

> window displays, changing two-dimensional art work, adult literacy tutoring, tutoring of school-age children, word processing and printing, photocopying, meeting rooms used for just about any non-profit group, staff fax for patrons (for a fee) . . . our outdoor sculpture that children climb on . . . live music occasionally, bulletin boards and brochure holders for library and non-library information . . . place to be out of the elements . . . a place to escape from unpleasant surroundings (a safe place). . .[3]

Academic libraries, too, can play that central role in their university and college communities and should look beyond their traditional roles and services to enhance those roles and services. In many cases, and certainly in the case of the university in which I work, a "virtual library" would be a cruel imposition on many of our students. Those who get all swivel-eyed about the prospects for the Net and the all-digital future seem to forget that many, many people live and work in circumstances that do not offer them a quiet place to study and think. For many such students, the library is the only place that is free from the distractions of everyday life, and in which assistance in their studies is freely available. To the affluent and the comfortable, quiet space is as available as air, and the concept of a home workstation connected to the world's "information" must seem affordable and attractive. To the poor and the struggling, such a setup would be unattainable, and replacing real libraries and real library service with electronics is yet another fantasy, another cruel hoax. It seems to me that we need more walls, not fewer—more library buildings with more to offer and not phantom libraries catering to alienated and isolated individuals bereft of human warmth and a human context.

The "Wired" Library as Place?

It is both easy and often done to accuse anyone who questions the digitization of everything of being antitechnology, as if the library as place were only defensible in nostalgic and romantic terms. There is, of course, something to be said for both nostalgia and romance, but the lack of universal availability of access to the Internet and electronic resources is creating yet another practical reason for preserving the library as place. On July 8, 1999, the U.S. Department of Commerce issued a report called *Falling through the Net: Defining the Digital Divide* that demonstrates that race, location, gender, age, and income are controlling factors in the question of access to electronic information resources.[4] Members of minority groups, the poor, the less educated, and disadvantaged children, particularly those who live in rural areas or in the inner city, are denied access at a time when the general population is joining the information age in droves. The answer, of course, is to use libraries, particularly public and school libraries, as centers of access to the Internet and places in which people can obtain instruction and assistance in the use of electronic resources. This may seem a peculiarly modern phenomenon, but there is a striking similarity to the history of the nineteenth-century public library in Britain and the United States. In the last third of that century, the rich had their books delivered to their houses, the upper middle class purchased their books from upscale bookshops, the middle class paid fees to borrow their books from private circulating libraries, and the legions of the working class used public libraries. The latter, besides providing wholesome recreation, became "the universities of the poor" and, often, a major path out of poverty.

The modern equivalent of the nineteenth-century public library could be the "wired library." (The latter is a common enough term, but one that could very soon be made obsolete by wireless technology.) A wired library is one that has incorporated into its place (housing all its nonelectronic programs and services) all the hardware and software that is necessary to gain access to a wide range of electronic services *and* provides instruction and assistance in their use, in addition to all other services.

My view of the wired library as place is that it could be as powerful a social force as were those early public libraries. This is not just for the simple reason that a library is a perfect place in which to provide a service in that it is usually centrally located and already contains professionals who are skilled in helping and advising seekers of information and knowledge. I believe there is a subtler reason. Wired libraries can demonstrate that access to electronic data and information is not the only way, or even, in many instances, the best way, to find the knowledge and information you need. It is true that many will come to, and bring their children to, a wired library because of the lure of free Internet access, but it is not difficult to see how innovative librarians can use that lure to open eyes to the wider picture. The idea of critical thinking is already commonplace in instruction programs in academic libraries, and the object of many such programs is as much to steer students away from the Net and the Web as it is to enable students to steer their way through them. How can a public or school library work to promote "traditional" library programs and services at the same time that it works to integrate electronic resources into those programs and services?

The first step is to ensure that everything about the library demonstrates the comprehensive nature of the service. Immediately on entering the library, even the first-time visitor should be able to see books, reading areas, terminals, and a reference/information desk or service point. Even someone who clearly has come to the library to use the Internet service should be aware of other services that are available. The second step is to work actively to promote the whole range of library services, particularly to the young. One ideal occurrence in a wired library would be to bring a class of young children to the library for a session introducing them to the Internet and then have them stay for story time. The third, and most important, step is to staff the wired library with librarians and other library workers who are technologically knowledgeable and enthusiastic about, and skilled in, the whole range of library collections and services.

Building the Ideal Twenty-first-century Library

The library building boom showed no sign of letting up at the end of the 1990s.

From more than 70 libraries in the United States, photographs flowed into *American Libraries*. Across the nation, libraries are doubling or quadrupling in size while adding computer stations, barrier free bathrooms, elevators, and fireplaces—or just opening new quarters.[5]

Despite the free-floating anxieties about the future of libraries, it seems that many communities, school districts, and universities and colleges are making long-term investments in the form of the construction of library buildings and the renovation and expansion of existing libraries. No community or institution makes such an investment on a whim. It is clear that this building is in response to the user community's call for expanded services and more suitable, and more inviting, library facilities. *Library Journal* reported that, between July 1996 and June 1997, there were 128 library renovation/expansion projects and 97 new libraries built for a total of 225 such public projects.[6] The renovations included the expansion of the Cleveland Public Library (at a cost of $67 million) and the lovely Multnomah County Central Library in Portland, Oregon ($25.7 million). Though many entirely new buildings are more expensive than renovation/expansion projects, it can be seen that the latter are not exactly cheap.

Given the fact that such massive expenditures of public funds have to be justified in terms of use over many years and given the perception that libraries are changing rapidly, it is more important than ever that such construction projects are carefully planned for the long haul.

New Issues

With reference to library buildings, some factors have been with us forever—materials storage, study areas, and so on. In building, expanding, or renovating library buildings for the twenty-first century, we face new issues that must be fitted into the complex of decisions to be made. They include:

- accommodating the disabled user
- creating the wired (or wireless) library
- providing for dual use

The Library and the Disabled User

The Americans with Disabilities Act (ADA) was signed into law in 1991 and all libraries have had to make adjustments of various kinds to ensure compliance with the act. I say "had to," but I am sure that those adjustments were welcomed by the great majority of librarians, not least because easy access to all is a common library value. There have been a number of articles and books on the ADA and there are official guidelines that have been used by many librarians and architects who are eager to ensure maximum accessibility for all. However, Karen Stone, in a brief but illuminating article written from the point of view of a wheelchair user, makes an eloquent plea for libraries to be planned in consultation with persons with disabilities on the very reasonable grounds that "what works for the disabled, works for others."[7] She describes a model library in a small town on the west coast of Sweden that provides effortless, easy access to "a totally integrated, relaxed environment." The ideal is, in her words, "universal access for the very small, the big, the blind, the deaf, the young, the old, the physically able and not-so-able, and more." Her fundamental point is that the Swedish library, and another that she praises in Corrales, New Mexico, were planned not just to conform to legal guidelines but also in consultation with people with disabilities. As Stone writes, "Asking 'what would be most useful for you?' is certainly cheaper and far more accurate than solely hiring non-disabled architects to analyze accessibility solutions." We should always communicate with users, but the need to do so in this case seems even more urgent than in others.

From Wire Less to Wired to Wireless

We have become used to the wired library (in the physical if not the metaphorical sense) and many of us have tried with great difficulty to deal with the problems of incorporating a telecommunications infrastructure into existing, aging structures. The Holy Grail used to be "the scholar's workstation"—a fixed, wired place that would deliver all the recorded knowledge and information to the researcher (as soon as that information had been digitized, of course). Most of us have fielded complaints about the fact that "there aren't enough terminals" and established sign-up systems for people to book a half-hour session at a terminal at peak times. Many new and renovated libraries have been fully wired at great expense. However, it seems that all those trials and efforts may soon be superseded by events. The "scholar's workstation" begins to look as quaint as Leonardo's flying machine and all that wiring may languish from disuse. It seems that we progressed from being unwired to wired and will soon progress to being wireless. The answer, for the present and near future at least, will be wireless networks within libraries (and beyond) accompanied by inexpensive and loaned "laptop" computers.[8] By these means, library users will be able to bring their own laptops into the library, or borrow laptops from the library, and have access to the library's online systems and electronic resources from anywhere in the library (or outside the library). Could it be that all those workstations and terminals will be consigned to the anteroom of history and replaced by brand new, spanking . . . library tables and carrels?!

Sharing Library Buildings

Another library building phenomenon of these days is that of dual use. By this I mean the new library building that shares a roof with other community facilities or with other kinds of libraries. At the very least, many new library buildings and extensions, while remaining primarily a particular kind of library facility, incorporate rooms and areas devoted to other purposes— community auditoria, meeting rooms, college computer labs, and so on (though note that wireless technology may well make computer labs obsolete). A project is under way to build a combined academic and public library on the campus of San Jose State University in San Jose, California.[9] The building will be funded and staffed jointly by the San Jose Public Library and San Jose State. This is a bold and exciting project that may well presage many future such developments, though the potential bureaucratic, logistic, economic, and administrative complexities are hair-raising. Another interesting recent example of dual use is the Carroll County Library and Senior Center in Mount Airy, Maryland.[10] This building houses a 17,000-square-foot library, and a 10,000-square-foot senior center, and a meeting room for nighttime community use. The library and the senior center are on different floors. There is no internal connection and each has its own entrance. One can see why the separation was desired but it does seem a pity that the users of the senior center have no convenient access to the library (given that the two almost certainly have an overlapping user group). Other dual-use projects involving public and academic libraries that are currently under consideration are those between the community library of Seminole, Florida, and the Seminole campus of St. Petersburg Junior College, and the proposed joint-use library by the Broward County (Florida) public library and Nova Southeastern University in Fort Lauderdale.[11] It is obvious that, in an age of escalating building costs, public and private institutions will look to creative and efficient collaboration as part of the solution to the library building problem.

What Will the Ideal Library Building of the Twenty-first Century Be Like?

Because of the range of types of libraries and the varying missions of those libraries, it is very difficult to prescribe the appearance and contents of the ideal library building. A new Library of Congress building will be as different from a new public library in a small Iowa town as the latter is from a major extension to a California academic library. All three have their own individual features, users, and purposes, but all are libraries—places dedicated to making recorded knowledge and information available to their users and providing appropriate services and space for that purpose. Where a commonality of purpose and function exists, there must be some basic similarities in the buildings in which those functions and purposes are to be effected.

External Appearance

Years ago, anyone could see that the design of libraries was heavily influenced by church architecture. From the choice of materials—often granite or another stone—to the style of architecture, many libraries built in the first half of the twentieth century clearly set out to impress, if not awe, at first sight. Public libraries built in the center of towns great and small, and college and university libraries built in the middle of campuses, had a solidity, magnificence, and sacred appearance that made it clear that here was something important, something to be reckoned with, something of permanence and permanent value. Inside, the church analogy seemed even stronger. Vaulted ceilings, dark woodwork, high windows—one was almost tempted to genuflect when approaching the card catalogue in the center of these magnificent edifices. Later generations took to using contemporary architectural fashions for new libraries. This was not always to great aesthetic effect. One acerbic critic said that the metal and glass "X Public Library and Information Center" built in Illinois in the 1970s should have been called the "X Public Library and Car Wash." (The offense was compounded by the fact that the new building replaced a lovely stone building in the Greek Revival style.) Another 1950s academic library in California has been described as looking like a Bulgarian police station. Sometimes, contemporary architecture is unappealing at first but proves to have enduring appeal over the decades. In other cases, the initial lack of appeal proves prophetic. The aesthetics of extensions to existing libraries are particularly tricky. The dilemma is, of course, whether to ape the original style and materials or to build something that harmonizes or to build something that is clearly different. Each of these can have both fortunate and unfortunate outcomes.

Another important matter about the outward appearance of a new or remodeled library is how it fits into the place in which it is situated—both in terms of the topography and the community served. In the words of one library architect:

> Each new or rehabilitated library needs to take into account what I call the community topography: that is, the particularities of the neighborhood it would serve.[12]

What we should seek (and often find) in a library building is harmony, both in terms of its appearance and its siting. This does not mean that each new library should be neoclassical or look as though it were designed by Thomas Jefferson. Modern architecture has brought us many fine buildings, and times and tastes change. However, harmony of appearance and harmony with its surroundings and purpose should be the minimal requirements of a new or remodeled library building. For a perfect match of harmony of appearance and harmony with its surroundings, see the perfectly lovely new neo–Prairie School public library building in Council Bluffs, Iowa.[13]

Inside the Library Building

Harmony and proportion should characterize the inside of the library building, too. Spaces should be easy to navigate for everyone (including the disabled) and should be suitable and adequate for their particular purpose. Furniture should be chosen with care, pleasing in appearance, and suited to its purpose. Light, natural and artificial, should be abundant but not glaring and should contribute to the aesthetic quality of the building. For a superb example of lighting created for a particular building and particular purpose, you need look no farther than the remodeled reading room of the New York Public Library, in which the lights are a distinct and positive design element. The colors and decorations of walls and ceilings, carpets and other floor coverings, artworks, plants, and other decorative elements are necessary features of public places. Those features must be chosen, planned for, and maintained as carefully as anything else in the building in order to preserve the harmony and aesthetics of the total space.

Library Materials

Two of the great breakthroughs in the democratization of library use were open stacks (accompanied by subject classification) and public access catalogues. The early open stacks held printed texts (books and bound journals) only. There was a reluctance to give the same access to newer forms of communication as they came along. There are reasons, in some cases, for segregating videos, audiotapes, CDs, and so on, but there is no reason at all that most of them should not be openly available to be browsed. There is certainly every reason why the records for electronic resources should be integrated into the online catalogue. By that means, a subject search yields not only a variety of titles but also a variety of materials—including electronic resources. This is not the place to discuss the cataloguing of electronic resources (see chapter 4), but suffice it to say that the fact that we cannot integrate electronic resources with the rest of the collection physically makes it even more important to integrate them into the catalogue. In the ideal library building, the physical collections will be easily available for perusal and use (irrespective of their format) and the intangible collections will be easily available through fixed terminals and portable devices.

The Use of Library Spaces

No matter whether you are dealing with a one-room library or the Library of Congress or all the libraries in between, there are certain uses for space that all have in common. All libraries use space to:

- house tangible materials and machines that give access to tangible and electronic resources (microform readers, computer terminals, etc.)
- provide study and consultation areas
- house a point of assistance (reference desk, etc.)
- provide places for staff to work

Individual libraries will contain special spaces for particular purposes. Typically, larger academic libraries will include rare book or special collections reading rooms, areas for format-specific collections (for example, maps, sound recordings, videos, microforms), areas for subject-specific collections (for example, law), and instructional rooms equipped with modern technology. Public libraries often contain separate children's sections, newspaper and magazine reading areas, and format-specific collections. It is impossible to generalize about special libraries, but they, too, depending on their subject coverage and clientele, will use space in particular ways. School libraries often include activity areas for class projects that are related to library use.

Children's Libraries

From one point of view, children's libraries are the most important libraries of all. They are places that provide the basis for lifelong literacy and learning, places that live in the memory long after we have ceased to be children. For that reason, it is very important that the space, furnishings, and so on allotted to the children's library do not just facilitate the efficient delivery of library service to children but also provide an environment of ease and peace that is conducive to the love of reading and learning. Children's libraries should be bright, welcoming, comfortable human spaces that children enjoy visiting and remaining in. Story times and other activities should intrigue and entice small children, and the children's library should be a place into which children can grow so that they keep returning long after they have outgrown story times (if we ever do!). I admire children's librarians and their unswerving devotion to service, their willingness to use every means to provide that service, and their openness to innovation (including technological innovation).

Housing Collections

The concept of open access to all library materials is, I believe, one of the controlling ideas of modern librarianship. Another is contained in one of Ranganathan's *Laws of Library Science*—"the library is a growing organism." Those two factors—open access and growth—involve many issues, the chief of which is space, which, for most libraries, translates into money. Open access demands far more space than closed access, and allowing for growth over a long period (remember there are no short periods in library lives) means that unfilled space has to be maintained for decades. Many of those who propose the virtual library base their arguments on the amount of space (and money) total digitization would save. By now, almost everyone agrees that we will never even come close to total digitization (and that it would not be desirable even if we did). Therefore, I would propose that we accept the need for expenditure on space and the creation of places called libraries, while using any means to lessen unnecessary space expenditures. Before we go on, it is important to recall that housing collections is not the only demand on library space, and that classrooms, study areas, reference areas, and so forth also consume considerable square footage in library buildings.

The new British Library in London—thirty-plus years in gestation and full the day it was opened—and the tragic San Francisco Public Library—famous for its concentration on technology at the expense of access to its collections—are salutary examples of the perils of ignoring Ranganathan's law. Buildings must be planned in such a way that the collections and services they house are able to grow over many decades. Some measures can be taken now, and new ideas and new technologies will undoubtedly offer more as libraries grow and change.

Compact, movable shelving has been shown in a variety of libraries and archives to be far more than a system of internal storage. These systems, which house more than three items in a space taken up by one in conventional, fixed shelving, are being widely used for open access with great success and, therefore, offer major space savings in new and refurbished library buildings. Another innovation of particular interest to academic libraries uses imaging systems to store back runs of periodicals, provide indexes to imaged databases, and print articles on demand. These are early days and such systems have only been demonstrated to work in a few small-scale projects, but it seems that technology may offer major space savings to libraries and an enhancement of service to their users. That is, of course, if they can be shown to be affordable and to provide archives of indefinite longevity.

The Place of Ideals

Library buildings come in all shapes and sizes. From the monumental to the unassuming, their styles and purposes are as varied as their communities of users. However, it is also true that all these buildings should embody enduring values—service, stewardship, the love of learning, and the others described in this book. A library building should work efficiently but it should also have higher qualities. It should be a place that inspires respect and encourages the pursuit of truth by scholars and children, by the high and the low, by the powerful and the powerless—because all these people come to the library with common aims and shared dreams. A library building should also be a good place in which to work, because harmony in the workplace generates joy in work, and joy in work leads to productive and effective service to society. The foregoing may seem impossibly idealistic and out of kilter in the age of technology and information. My answer is a question: Without ideals and values, what is the point? The truth is that we all seek meaning in all aspects of our lives, and the creation and maintenance of useful, harmonious library places and spaces is a crucial step toward finding meaning in our work as librarians.

NOTES

1. *Institutions as a Fulcrum for Change,* Partners for Livable Communities (Washington, D.C., 1996), quoted in Neal Pierce, "The Magic of Community Assets," *National Journal* (September 21, 1996): 1707.

2. Pierce, "The Magic of Community Assets."

3. Personal communication from Evelyn Murphy (Newton, Iowa, Public Library).

4. *http://www.ntia.doc.gov/ntiahome/digitaldivide/*

5. "The Boom Goes On," *American Libraries* 30, no. 4 (April 1999): 52.

6. Bette-Lee Fox and Maya L. Kremen, "The Renovation Model," *Library Journal* 122, no. 20 (December 1997): 49–62.

7. Karen G. Stone, "To Roll into a Library," *American Libraries* 27, no. 5 (May 1996): 41–42.

8. Surely this name will change—the only place I have ever seen the devices on laps is on an airplane.

9. George M. Eberhart, "Three Plans for Shared Use Libraries in the Works," *American Libraries* 30, no. 1 (January 1999): 21.

10. Vernon Mays, "Double Duty," *Architecture* 84, no. 6 (June 1995): 84–88.

11. Eberhart, "Three Plans."

12. Francis Murdock Pitts, "What to Read When Building a Library (or, Is That a Mastodon in the Choir Loft)," *American Libraries* 27, no. 4 (April 1996): 48–51.

13. Will Manley, "Keeping Up with the Times," *American Libraries* 30, no. 8 (September 1999): 144.

4

Stewardship

Littera scripta manet.[1]

What Is the Meaning of Stewardship?

Steward is a word that derives from two Old English words meaning "house" and "warden"—that is, someone with responsibility for ensuring the safety and orderly functioning of a house or, by extension, any small community. It is still found in that narrow meaning in such phrases as "airline steward." Its wider, metaphorical meaning goes back, at least, to the King James Bible and refers to someone or some entity that preserves the value of something and ensures that future generations enjoy the legacy that comes to them with an equal or enhanced value as a result of that stewardship.[2] Someone who inherits an estate and improves it during the period he or she is a guardian before giving it to inheritors can fairly be said to have exercised stewardship.

What Is the Relation between Stewardship and Libraries?

Stewardship in the library context has three components:

1. the preservation of the human record to ensure that future generations know what we know

2. the care and nurture of education for librarianship so that we pass on our best professional values and practices

3. the care and maintenance of our libraries so that we earn the respect of our communities

Preserving the Records of Humankind

The task of the librarian, then, is to rescue the past for the enlightenment of the present, to preserve the past not for its own sake or for the curiosity of the antiquarian, but for the meaning it has for today and tomorrow.[3]

The inheritance of which we are stewards is no less than the complete cultural and historical legacy of the records of humankind. The value of stewardship is one of our most important duties and burdens—one that we must honor if we are to carry out our mission of preserving the human record and transmitting it to future generations. It is interesting to see how infrequently the question of preserving recorded knowledge and information in digital form is raised during discussions of the future of libraries. If raised, the question is usually dismissed as something that technology and cooperative action will solve as if by magic at some yet to be determined time. Somehow, it seems that historic role of libraries is being ignored, simply because even all-digital enthusiasts understand the immense practical and technological problems posed by digital archives.

Librarians and archivists (whom I regard as members of the same church, if often in schism!) have a unique role in preserving and transmitting the records of humankind on behalf of future generations. I do not use the word "unique" lightly. Many of our values and missions are shared with other groups and interests, but we alone are dedicated to the preservation of recorded knowledge and information. Publishers, booksellers, teachers, researchers, museum keepers are among the people who benefit directly from the fact that the records of the past are available to them, but only librarians and archivists are engaged in the wholesale preservation of those records. If a substantial amount of the world's recorded knowledge and information were to be available in digital form, and only in digital form, we would be facing a crisis in the preservation of the human record that would dwarf anything that we have seen since the dawn of the age of printing. It is imperative that librarians work together to produce a grand plan for future stewardship that contains practical and cost-effective means of ensuring that future generations are able to know what we know.

The Electronic Age?

Some say that the age of print will, at some time in the future, yield to the electronic age. In contemplating that possibility, it is instructive to look at the transition to the age of print from the age that preceded it—the age of script. Thomas Jefferson wrote,

> How many of the precious works of antiquity were lost while they existed only in manuscript? Has there ever been one lost since the art of printing has rendered it practicable to multiply and disperse copies? This leads us then to the only means of preserving those remains of our laws . . . that is, a multiplication of printed copies.[4]

In her magisterial work on the transformational effect of printing, Elizabeth Eisenstein discusses three attributes of the printed book that distinguished it sharply from the manuscript or, to use her terms, distinguish the print culture from the script culture. They are *standardization, dissemination,* and *fixity.* In many ways, her analysis of the script culture closely parallels a modern analysis of what I will call, for the sake of symmetry, the electronic culture. This is especially true in the case of fixity. Manuscripts of the same "work" differed greatly one from the other to the same degree that various versions of electronic texts differ from other versions—for the same reason (each copyist introduced change and error) and with the same deleterious effect. It is always tempting to see the history of human communication as one of constant progress. Humankind has advanced from no recorded communication in prehistorical days through a variety of media from clay tablets and stone to paper and electronics, each medium being more extensive and less durable than its predecessor. Because of the increasing numbers of communications made possible by new media and because we retain the older media for the sake of their durability (using, for example, stone for memorials and vellum for important historical documents), it is tempting to buy the "onward and upward" theory. Could it be that the story is not one of progress? Could it be that future historians of communication (if there be any such) might look back on the five-hundred-plus-year period that began with Gutenberg and ended (on some as yet undetermined date) with the "triumph" of electronic technology as an aberration—an island of fixity and transmission of the human record arising from the swamp of the age of script and declining into the electronic swamp? Adrian Johns ties print to such concepts as "veracity" and "civility."[5] The point is that the stability of print and the standardization of publishing created an intellectual climate in which there is a bond of trust between the author, publisher, and reader. That implicit contract has the following parts:

> A book published by a reputable publisher is what it says it is.
>
> Reputable publishers publish books that can be trusted.
>
> A book by a reputable author contains facts that have been verified to the best of the author's, editor's, and publisher's ability.
>
> A book by a reputable author contains opinions and interpretations that are the author's *or* are clearly labeled as the opinions or interpretations of others.
>
> Citations, sources, and the rest of the scholarly apparatus in a book published by a reputable publisher clearly indicate the origins of the facts and opinions contained in that book.
>
> Each manifestation of a clearly labeled edition of a text is identical to all other manifestations of that edition.

Not a single one of those elements of the unwritten contract between publishers, authors, and readers is present in the electronic world of today and the foreseeable future. There is nothing to stop anyone from gaining access to any electronic document and changing it to his or her heart's delight before disseminating it as something it is not. That is the heart of the dilemma faced by authors and readers in an electronic world devoid of fixity, standardization, and verifiable veracity.

Stewardship of the Human Record in Action

How, then, should we exercise stewardship over the records of humanity? The simple answer, and the truest, is that we should do everything that we can to preserve significant recorded knowledge and information in such a manner that it is available not just to the next generation, or even the next few generations, but for the indefinite future. The key word in the foregoing sentence is "significant." One of the ironies of the present predicament in preservation is that we have solved the issue without having to make the kind of value judgment that "significant" implies. It is beyond question that the best, indeed the only proven, way to preserve recorded knowledge and information is to print it on acid-free paper, make many copies, bind those copies well, and distribute them to libraries throughout the world. In that system, it is the publisher or printer or both who make the judgment. After that decision to print, publish, and distribute, the rest is automatic. There has never been any better preservation system and it imposes very little on libraries apart from the expense, the considerable expense, of providing space for all those bound volumes. I will return to the question of value judgments based on assessment of "significance" later but, first, wish to sketch the preservation issues that face each broad medium of communication today.

BOOKS AND PRINTED JOURNALS

There are a number of enemies of print on paper, including damp, heat, quality of paper, and inappropriate or poor binding. That being said, there are two massive advantages: (1) the many duplicates of each publication and (2) the seemingly limitless life of a well-bound text printed on acid-free paper and preserved in favorable conditions.

MANUSCRIPTS

These are the mirror images of books in that drawings and writings on paper and other media are, by definition, unique, and very likely to have been stored, for at least some of their existence, in less than optimal conditions. I well remember the collection of the manuscripts of a world-famous poet with which I had the pleasure of working. Many drafts of the poems were written on the backs of bill envelopes, and the collection had been stored in various boxes made for holding shoes and comestibles and transported from one venue to another in the course of a peripatetic and adventurous life. Technology, particularly optical disc technology, offers means of preserving, protecting, and disseminating unique manuscript collections.

MAPS AND MUSIC SCORES

Many of the circumstances that apply to printed books apply to these materials, but it should be noted that single maps are more fragile than printed books and many maps and scores exist in fewer copies than do books.

SOUND RECORDINGS

It has been said that each successive medium of sound recording is more durable than its predecessor. From wires to wax cylinders to 78s to tapes of various kinds to EPs, LPs, and now digital tape and compact discs, it appears that we have moved from the fragile to the indestructible. That may be so and perhaps CDs really are invulnerable to time and use. A cautious person will note that we have no proof of the longevity of CDs and also that any medium that is based on a playing technology is subject not only to damage to that medium but also to the future availability of the playing machines. My grandmother had a phonograph with a horn on which she used to play her 78s of the beloved Irish tenor Count John McCormack. It seems entirely possible that our sleek CD players of today will look as quaint and be as unavailable in 2050 as her phonograph looks and is today.

FILMS AND VIDEOS

I have heard that fully one-third of the feature films made in the one-hundred-year history of moving pictures are gone forever. A segment on preservation on the American Movie Classics television channel states that half the American feature films made before 1950 no longer exist.[6] Of those that remain, many are on film that is brittle, is in colors that have faded, or depends on a process or projector that is no longer available. We have seen a number of video formats fail (U-Matic, Beta, and DVXs, for example) and others (VHS, videodiscs, DVDs) survive, at least for the moment. It is hardly likely that all or any of the currently used video formats (and the machines on which they are played) will be around, say, fifteen years from now.

ARTIFACTS AND ARTWORKS

Many libraries contain artifacts and artworks that embody or contain recorded knowledge and information. The wise librarian takes guidance from museums, art galleries, and other specialists on the preservation and special treatment of such materials.

MICROFORMS

The story of microfilm, microfiche, microcards, micro-opaques, and the other variations of the medium that first surfaced during the Franco-Prussian War of 1870 is salutary. For most of this century, microforms have been perceived as the salvation of libraries in terms of library space and of preservation. One variation—ultrafiche—contained so many images that it was predicted we would all be "carrying the Library of Congress around in a briefcase." Nice try. Microforms have several drawbacks, chief among them the fact that library users hate them. There is also the instability of some earlier forms of microfilm; the lack of standardization of reading machines for some microforms (microcards, ultrafiche, and the like); and doubts about the long-term durability of even the established microforms.

DIGITAL RESOURCES

There are so many intractable issues concerning the preservation of digitized recorded knowledge and information and so few proposed practical solutions that it is tempting to do what many digital enthusiasts have done—ignore them. However, it may be worth listing some issues here.

> The vast majority of digital information is worthless, of only temporary usefulness, or of very local interest. How is all that chaff to be separated from the worthwhile wheat? And who will undertake that labor of Hercules?

> The hardware used to gain access to digital information changes radically quite frequently—this means that preservation programs must also involve considerations of the hardware needed for access.

> Even selective digital archives will be massive. Who is to ensure that governments and organizations will maintain those archives for centuries in the future?

Which Documents Are "Significant"?

This is a difficult and, in many ways, unanswerable question. As I have pointed out previously, librarians have largely left it to publishers and booksellers and, to a lesser extent, to the law and to library book vendors. After all, it is not librarians who decide what is or is not to be published and what is or is not a legal publication. Add to that our almost universally held belief that library users are entitled to everything that is available and you can readily see us as professionals who are reluctant to employ such criteria as significance and worth. All libraries, great and small, practice some degree of selection but that selection is, first, from a known and limited universe—the universe of published items—and, second, mostly confined to questions of suitability for the community that the library serves. In short, most librarians not only do not practice selection based on the significance or value of one publication as compared to another but also actively shy away from such questions for fear of being accused of censorship. There is one shining exception to this pattern—the children's librarian. I have always admired children's librarians for many reasons—chief among them being their willingness to distinguish between "good" books and those that are inferior and to make selection choices based on their principles and values. The rest of us are reluctant and, anyway, out of practice. What then are we to do when faced with the Internet and electronic resources of all kinds? There are really only three basic strategies and none of them cause the librarian's heart to leap with joy.

1. We can ignore the question and give as much access to as much stuff as we can without regard to value. This, of course, means ceding the preservation issue before we start.

2. We can choose the electronic resources that we buy or, more likely, lease with care and choose the links we make from our Web page with care and simply not bother about the rest of the electronic swamp.

3. We can consciously set out to choose, evaluate, give access to, and preserve those things that we find significant and of value. A noble endeavor but one that calls for expenditures few of us are prepared to make, is based on the exercise of skills that few of us possess, and requires policies that none of us has, as yet, formulated.

To illustrate how tricky such discriminations can be in the electronic realm, we need look no farther than two examples from the orderly world of print.

Two decades ago, *New Yorker* writer Frances Fitzgerald published a fascinating book about the way in which the United States constantly revises its history.[7] This influential and widely read work was based almost entirely on the study of high school textbooks from the past one hundred years. There must be few academic librarians who would put outdated schoolbooks high on their lists of significant types of publication.

As I write, the West is dealing with the aftermath of the dissolution of the state of Yugoslavia. The deliberate attempt to obliterate the civic identity of those being ethnically cleansed was part of those melancholy events. Librarians at the University of Michigan and elsewhere have made a concerted attempt to collect Yugoslavian telephone books from the past twenty years to help the United Nations verify the identities of returning refugees and, thus, restore their civil and civic rights.

So, *schoolbooks* are a valuable research resource and *telephone books* are vital historical records in an unhappy land. There are abundant other examples of the significance of the insignificant, and they all illustrate the immensity of the problem. That immensity should not discourage us from attempting to be good stewards of all our records (including electronic records). On the contrary, it should energize us in our pursuit of the twin goals of preserving what we have and establishing systems that will enable us to preserve the future records of humankind.

The Modern Language Association, in a statement issued in 1995, reaffirmed the continuing importance of the book and its primary role in scholarly enquiry.[8] Though we all play a part in the preservation and provision of books, the fact is that the multimillion-volume research library has the lead role in that endeavor. Despite all the talk about migration to electronic resources, as Stephen Enniss asks, which research library "has stopped buying and adding books?"[9] He states the need for scholars and librarians to fight the overwhelming problems posed by books printed on acidic paper and by neglect based on a shift of perception about the importance of books. Further, he notes a species of mental judo in the discussion of preserving the total scholarly record that shifts from the problems of preserving print on paper to those of preserving electronic resources. They are, of course, quite different and pose different questions demanding different answers. We have done a fairly good job over the centuries of preserving almost everything of value in the print record. Absent malice and malevolent neglect, there is no reason why that almost total success rate should not continue. On the other hand, we have scarcely even begun to preserve electronic resources. Vague plans have been drawn up and much has been said and little done. Success in that preservation effort is, at best, a very long shot indeed.

Beyond the Preservation of the Human Record

In his seminal article, Lee Finks defines stewardship as "a responsibility for the destiny of the library as an institution."[10] He stresses that the survival of the library and its collections is crucial to the destiny of culture and society. This grand task is obviously centered on the preservation of the human record but also involves the survival and development of the library and of librarianship. In my opinion, that latter mission has two important components:

> preserving the knowledge of librarianship for future generations of librarians by means of library education
>
> assuring the bond of trust between the library and the society we serve by demonstrating our stewardship and commitment, thus strengthening the mutuality of the interests of librarians and the wider community

The second component depends on us acting with responsibility and ethics in the service of our particular community and of society as a whole. We have the implicit respect of most of the people we serve, which is a good foundation. However, that generalized good feeling needs to be intensified if it is to be of practical use. If we are to continue to earn the respect and support of our communities, we must demonstrate that our mission is relevant to their lives and to the wider culture. There is no better way to do that than to make that mission plain and to work hard on being good servants of the culture and good stewards of its records.

Library Education

I honestly believe that libraries, on the whole, are doing a good job of preserving the records of humankind. I also believe that a certain lack of assertion is our only failing in demonstrating to our communities that we are good stewards. Modesty is an admirable trait, but excessive modesty can be a political mistake of the first order. We do good work and should not be afraid to proclaim it, especially to those who fund our activities. Library education, on the other hand, is a disaster that is in danger of becoming a catastrophe.

There are many villains and numerous failures in the sad story of American library education. Practitioners blame educators. Educators blame practitioners. Teachers, students, practitioners, the American Library Association (ALA) and other professional organizations, and writers of books and articles on libraries are all complicit in this train wreck. Almost the entire debate centers on "the 'L' word" (an annoying trope modeled on euphemisms for curse words) referring to the growing number of "library schools" that do not use the word "library" in their name. This last is a particularly fatuous thing to do as most of the renamed schools produce graduates who seek employment in libraries. (The sole exception thus far is the once storied school at the University of California, Berkeley, which, under the leadership of a microeconomist, has formally abandoned the teaching of librarianship.) Though such semantic discussion is as futile as it appears, it is symbolic of the deep ill, the existential crisis, that has gripped our profession. (It is odd, is it not, that some librarians are fleeing from the word "library" as outmoded, when computer types happily use the word "computer" for the machines that are far more than the calculators the name implies?[11]) Speaking for myself, I have lived most of my life as a librarian, love libraries, and will die proud of having been a librarian, without ever wishing to change the word "library" or any of its cognates.

The sad facts behind the "L word" wars are these:

> A huge gulf exists between the interests of library educators and library practitioners.
>
> Three of the former intellectual powerhouses of American librarianship (the schools at Columbia, Chicago, and Berkeley) are dead or malignly transformed.
>
> Many library school graduates lack basic education in the central processes of librarianship.
>
> Many library schools contain two, mutually irreconcilable cultures—a (female-dominated) culture of librarianship and a (male-dominated) information science culture.[12]
>
> Many practitioners and employers cannot or will not accept their role of training new librarians and fail to distinguish between education and training.
>
> The ALA accreditation process has become a farce.

Let us go to the basic issue. An enlightened employer—the consumer of the product of the library schools—wishes to hire librarians who have been educated in the core competences of our profession. Much has been made of the difficulty of determining which those core areas are. I think that is an insupportable argument. Is there a single employer in a library of any kind who wishes to hire someone in a professional position who lacks an education in any one of the following—bibliographic control, reference work, collection development, library systems, and electronic resources? I have noted previously that "education" is the key word here—not "training." It is the role of the enlightened employer to provide training in, say, cataloguing, reference work, or collection development, but even the most enlightened employer cannot do that in the absence of a foundation of understanding provided by a good education. One complaint heard frequently now concerns the difficulty of hiring new cataloguers, now that many library schools no longer require cataloguing courses. I think this is a small part of the problem. The absence of new cataloguers causes difficulties but it is nowhere near as grave a problem as the huge number of new librarians in any sphere who do not understand the architecture of bibliographic control and, therefore, cannot function properly as reference librarians, collection development librarians, or any other kind of librarian.[13] *US News and World Report* unwittingly told the sad truth when it headlined an article on library education "The Modern MLS Degree: Library Schools Today Are Turning Out Webmasters."[14] Exactly. How many Webmasters does a library need? The answer, I suspect, is somewhere between one and none.

Information Science and What It Has Wrought

The adverse impact of information science on library schools cannot be overstated. Although a sadly overlooked article demonstrated and documented the fact that there is really no such thing as "information science," this bogus discipline has a stranglehold on many of our library schools.[15] Many of the courses that would add to the education of librarians are being elbowed out by IS courses that have little or no relevance to the real work of real librarians in real libraries. The reason for this is that academics (mostly male academics) are pursuing their own interests, grants, and promotion or tenure at the expense of useful library education. Many of them are not librarians or have little interest in libraries and their mission—indeed, think that the library has no future. It is a free country and everyone is entitled to his or her views—no matter how wrongheaded. However, people with those beliefs should found their own schools and not work to the detriment of the suppliers of future librarians. If the profession is weakened and sickened in this manner, our mission of preserving "the library and its fruits" (Lee Finks' words) will fail.

Accreditation

In 1992, the American Library Association changed its standards on accreditation of library schools and, in my view, weakened library education and the library profession.[16] The accreditation process, essentially, now works like this. The persons designated by ALA's Committee on Accreditation ask the library school what it is trying to accomplish and then assess how well it is doing in that self-defined task. So, if the School of Information Studies at X University states that it is in the business of "educating information professionals for the new millennium" and that process does not involve the study of bibliographic control but does involve Webmastery, that school will be judged on how well it produces Webmasters. In this way, the American *Library* Association is saying, in essence, "Teach what you like and we will still certify your graduates as worthy to be employed in libraries." Almost all advertisements for new library positions contain the magic words "MLS (or equivalent) from an ALA-accredited school." Until the past decade, a prospective employer could assume a common body of knowledge in an applicant who was a graduate of an ALA-accredited school. No longer. Because ALA turned the process into what amounts to self-accreditation, the alert employer needs to look at the degree (by no means are all master's degrees from library schools the "equivalent" of an MLS), the school, and the school's curriculum—all of which is more work than we are used to.

It is difficult to imagine the American Medical Association accrediting a medical school that allowed its graduates to become doctors without having studied surgery. It is equally difficult to imagine the American Bar Association looking with approval on a law school that neither taught nor intended to teach constitutional law. Why, then, is no one puzzled by ALA's acceptance of library schools that do not require their graduates to have more than the most elementary knowledge of cataloguing?

The recent Congress on Professional Education convened by ALA (invitation only) reached a crossroad of wildly antithetical modes of proceeding. A number of recommendations emerged from the Congress and are the present study of a number of ALA-appointed task forces, committees, and the like. I would like to concentrate on two of those recommendations. The report of the Congress's steering committee contains the following:

... the ALA, in consultation with the appropriate partner group(s), must ...

1.2. identify the core competencies for [*sic*] the profession

- a clear statement of competencies should be available to educators, practitioners, and the public; while there has been concern expressed about the lack of attention to particular core competencies, there is a statement of core competencies in the current (1992) Standards for Accreditation, these need to be affirmed and profiled, or *reconsidered and revised* [my emphasis] ...

and

2.1. explore the possibility of an independent board for Accreditation

- ... it is critical that discussions be held to explore the feasibility of a collaborative, independent board comprising, and supported by, all the primary players, including ALA ...[17]

In other words, the committee is planning to address the crisis in library education by

(a) devising and revising the list and description of the areas of study that are essential to the education of a librarian (the "core competencies"), and

(b) weakening ALA's already tenuous, nay invisible, control over what is taught in library schools by ceding its powers of accreditation to another body on which ALA is but one "player."

What is the point of a list of "core competencies" if there is no mechanism to ensure that they are taught in library schools and that library school graduates possess them on graduation? Why would a major professional association wish to surrender control (even theoretical control) over the education of its members to a mishmash of other "players"?

Accreditation is in crisis in other ways. Library schools have died, faded away, or become something else. Others are said to be on the verge of leaving the accreditation process ("information science"–saturated Indiana and Syracuse head most lists). This is generally assumed to be a very bad thing and library education to be on the verge of suffering mortal wounds. It may well be, but not because of high-profile defections. After all, the last crisis in library education was supposed to be fatal because fifteen library schools folded between 1978 and 1993—including the famous examples of Columbia and Chicago. They are much missed, but life goes on and what ails today's library schools has little to do with the absence of those fifteen schools. My guess is that the same would apply if other big-name schools walked the information science plank. The key issue for them would be the employment prospects of their graduates who wish to work in libraries. Perhaps there will be none such and the defectors will, like Berkeley, cease to be library schools in fact as well as in name. On the other hand, I do hope that a "library school" that walked away from accreditation would not expect its graduates to be considered for jobs for which an "MLS (or equivalent) from an ALA-accredited school" is a requirement.

Another problem with accreditation today is the perception that the Committee on Accreditation (COA) carries out its work inconsistently and in the shadows. Two recent denials of accreditation (Denver and Arizona) have mystified many. Also, instances of schools being accredited for three or four years (instead of the standard seven) without satisfactory explanation have created a climate of distrust and lack of communication.

Accreditation is at the heart of professional identity and the connection between practitioners and education. Yet it is ailing, weak, and confused. Few librarians really understand the accreditation process, but they do understand its effect on new colleagues (and the lack of new colleagues). If the system collapsed or was outsourced or just faded away, where would we be? In that dread future, we would find ourselves trying to weigh the suitability of a person with an "MLS" from Podunk State's School of Information Economics against that of someone with a "Master's of Information Management" from the Millard

Fillmore College's School of Library and Media Center Studies. In a world in which no school is accredited, all schools are accredited. That is why our stewardship of our profession must revivify library education by

> defining the core of our profession and the necessary penumbral skills and knowledge;
>
> creating a core curriculum;
>
> accrediting MLS (or equivalent) programs—rather than library schools—on the basis of how well they teach that core curriculum; and
>
> ensuring that the accreditation process is firmly in the hands of ALA and is carried out by the successor to COA in an explicit, standardized, clearly understood, and overt manner.

Being a Good Steward

If we are to succeed, individually and collectively, as stewards of the human record and our profession, we will do three things:

1. Ensure that future generations know what we know by designing and implementing effective collaborative schemes to preserve recorded knowledge and information, irrespective of format. In particular, resolve the problem of controlling and preserving significant electronic resources.
2. Do good work and earn the trust and respect of the communities we serve.
3. Revive, strengthen, and maintain library education by defining our profession, ensuring that library schools educate new librarians according to an agreed core curriculum, and devising an effective an fair accreditation system controlled by ALA.

NOTES

1. "The written word remains"—Horace.
2. Luke 16.
3. Jesse H. Shera, "Apologia pro Vita Nostra," in his *Knowing Books and Men: Knowing Computers Too* (Littleton, Colo.: Libraries Unlimited, 1973), 120.
4. Quoted in Elizabeth Eisenstein, *The Printing Press as an Agent of Change*, vol. 1 (Cambridge: Cambridge University Pr., 1979), 115–116.

5. Adrian Johns, *The Nature of the Book* (Chicago: University of Chicago Pr., 1998).

6. Heard Monday, July 19, 1999.

7. Frances Fitzgerald, *America Revised: History Schoolbooks in the Twentieth Century* (Boston: Little, Brown, 1979).

8. "MLA Statement on the Significance of Primary Records," in *Profession 95* (New York: MLA, 1995), 27–28.

9. Stephen Enniss, "Collaborative Values and the Survival of the Print Record," *C&RL News* 60, no. 6 (June 1999): 459–460, 464.

10. Lee W. Finks, "Values without Shame," *American Libraries* (April 1989): 352–356.

11. *Compute:* To determine by calculation; to reckon. *Webster's New Collegiate Dictionary* (1953).

12. Suzanne Hildenbrand, "The Information Age versus Gender Equity?" *Library Trends* 47, no. 4 (spring 1999): 669–681.

13. Michael Gorman, "How We Should Teach Cataloguing and Classification," in *AACR, DDC, MARC, and Friends* (London: Library Association, 1993).

14. Marissa Melton, "The Modern MLS Degree: Library Schools Today Are Turning Out Web-masters," *U.S. News and World Report,* March 29, 1999. http://*www.usnews.com/usnews/edu/ beyond/grad/gbmls.htm*

15. Lloyd Houser, "A Conceptual Analysis of Information Science," *Library and Information Science Research* 10 (January 1988): 3–34.

16. American Library Association, Committee on Accreditation, *Standards for Accreditation* (Chicago: ALA, 1992).

17. "Report of the Steering Committee on [*sic*] the Congress for Professional Education" (June 1999). *www.ala.org/congress/cope_report.html*

5

Service

What Is the Meaning of Service?

"Service" is a complex word with many meanings and nuances within meanings. For example, *Webster's Third* contains twenty main definitions of the word "service"—most with a number of subdefinitions.[1] The definitions that best express my interpretation of service are

> duty done or required;
>
> professional or other useful ministrations;
>
> effort inspired by philanthropic motives or dedicated to human welfare or betterment.

Read those last few words carefully because they sum up the ethos, motivation, and goals of our profession. In doing that, they make the case that a profession based on service is an altruistic profession. Our desire is to serve individuals and, in doing so, to serve society and humanity as a whole.

What Is the Relation between Service and Libraries?

Without being pious, one can state that the concept of the duty and service inspired by professional values and a desire to better humankind can be a guiding light for all librarians and library policies. Conversely, it is hard to imagine a productive and effective library that is not imbued with the idea of service or to envisage a happy work life for an individual in such a library.

Librarianship is a profession defined by service. Every aspect of librarianship, every action that we take as librarians can and should be measured in terms of service. It is important to get away from the negative aspects and definitions of the word (it is unfortunate, in this respect, that "service" has cognates with such associations as "servile" and "servant"). Our service can be as large as a successful integration of library instruction with the undergraduate curriculum or as small as a single brief act of helpfulness to a catalogue user. Whichever it is, the value of service can and should pervade our professional lives so that it becomes the yardstick by which we measure all our plans and projects and the means by which we assess success or failure of all our programs. A library three-year plan that measured any proposed change or innovation against its impact on service to that library's users would be successful. Any such plan that ignored service would fail.

Service in Action

One of the most important changes in the wider economy, and one with great implications for society, has been the change from an industrial economy to a service economy. Nearly three-quarters of the people in the American labor force work in services; nearly half of family incomes is spent on services; and good service is seen to be an important criterion in judging the effectiveness of all organizations.[2] Many things that used to be made *in* the developed world are now made *for* the developed world in less-developed countries. Car salespersons are more easily found than car mechanics, and communities that used to supply muscle power for a manufacturing industry are now facing the difficult transition, through retraining, to supplying service workers. In the new economy, the search for a service edge is an intense part of competition, especially when the service deals with commonly encountered goods. To put it bluntly, in the rare cases in which a company is the *only* supplier of a widely consumed item, cost and service are of marginal importance. The much more common situation, however, is that of competition between companies that sell similar fast food and sodas, similar inexpensive clothing, seats in identical multiplex cinemas, and all the other homogenous items consumed by an increasingly homogenous society. The edge is to be found in two areas—price and service. It is striking that many of the most successful companies, nationally and globally, are noted for their service and attention to the individual customer. Further, that emphasis is growing as it becomes more difficult to find striking price differences in bands of company type (inexpensive apparel, chain restaurants, video stores, personal computer vendors, etc.).

Improvements and innovations in service in the commercial world have been achieved by two, sometimes antithetical, means—technology and human contact. Well-designed technology can lead to great increases in service and consequent customer satisfaction. The more successful enterprises in electronic commerce (such as Amazon.com) are eloquent testimonials to technology-driven service. On the other hand, technology used to replace human contact for cost-cutting reasons (electronic banking, seemingly endless multiple choice telephone systems, etc.) has, in many cases, led to a customer backlash. In those instances, customers perceived the elimination of the human factor as a loss of service and have often caused companies to reverse their strategy.

The vast majority of libraries operate in the public sector and, even when they do not, are seldom judged in terms of price. (They are increasingly subject to cost-efficiency and cost-benefit assessment, but that is different from being concerned with the unit price of services.) Of the two ways to get an edge, therefore, service is the one that applies to most of us. We, too, have to balance technology and the human factor in our drive to achieve better levels of service.

The test of service in libraries lies not in its definition or philosophical underpinnings but in our practical applications of that value. To understand those practical applications, we have to create and apply evaluative procedures. There are many ways to measure service (number of reference questions answered, number of book requests filled within two months, etc.) but some dimensions of service—particularly those connected with the human element—are not nearly as quantifiable as others. Measuring the quantity of reference questions answered is infinitely easier than measuring the quality of those answers. Measuring the number of students reached by a library instruction program is a cakewalk compared to assessing the outcomes of that instruction. In libraries as in all aspects of life, it is easier to count items than to assess quality.[3] This is not to say that we should abandon the attempt to evaluate in terms of quality, but to emphasize that human-to-human transactions are, by definition, complex and multidimensional.

What is the universe of service in libraries? It is all too easy to concentrate on the service element in what most libraries used to call "public services"—reference service, branch library service, special and subject library work. We should not forget that service may be direct or indirect, and that a service rendered indirectly is equal in importance to direct human-to-human service.

Technical Service

A technical processing operation that identifies the materials needed by library users and ensures speedy and timely accession and cataloguing to make those materials available for use is just as much in the business of service as is a busy reference desk. Indirect service by technical processing is also just as involved with the human aspect of library use as is a more direct public service unit. Ensuring that library users have timely access to the materials they want is an important component of the service role of the library. So is the construction of user-friendly bibliographic control systems that enable users to locate materials they need. In the past, it was too easy for bibliographic control work and systems work to become ends in themselves, without regard for the users of catalogues and online systems—thus leading to the stereotypes of the rule-obsessed cataloguer and the technology-obsessed library techie. I am certain that, for a variety of reasons, those attitudes are fading and user-friendly systems are becoming commonplace, as are service-oriented procedures in processing and systems. The service rendered by technical processing and systems units includes the following:

> selecting appropriate materials for library collections
>
> working with materials vendors to establish plans to ensure the speedy delivery of needed items, both classes of material and individual orders
>
> establishing contracts for access to remote electronic resources
>
> cataloguing and classifying materials using national and international standards to make them accessible to library users
>
> building and maintaining local catalogues and contributing quality bibliographic data to regional, national, and other shared databases
>
> contributing to the design and implementation of advanced, user-friendly online systems that integrate access to a wide variety of resources

Reference Service and the Service Encounter

At the heart of every service is the service encounter. Everything flows from it. A service encounter is the event at which a customer comes into contact with a service provider, its people, its communications and other technology, and the service it provides. . . . [I]t has been termed . . . "the moment of truth."[4]

Just as in a commercial service enterprise, it is easier to see the direct service element than to discern the many activities of those in "back rooms." It is easier to grasp the service dimension of reference services than it is almost any other library activity. Though those services have expanded beyond "the person at the reference desk," they still maintain that vital component of human interaction—that "moment of truth"—at the center of their service.

One text contains a service matrix of which the axes are willingness/ unwillingness to serve and ability/inability to serve, leading to four categories of service personnel: those who are willing and able; those who are willing but unable; those who are able but unwilling; and those who are unwilling and unable.[5] Good management is aimed at getting all personnel into the first category and discovering, as a preliminary to retraining and reorientation, why the negative characteristics of those in the other three categories exist. As the quotation at the beginning of this section points out, the person delivering a service represents the whole entity (the service provider), and the provider (the library in this case) is judged by the qualities (positive and negative) of that person.

As has been shown in many department stores, banks, travel agencies, and other commercial concerns, people in need of assistance want the person from whom they seek help to be

- approachable,
- knowledgeable, and
- comprehensible.

Approachability does not involve the mindless friendliness of the "have a nice day" variety, but it is seriously compromised by a grim or arrogant demeanor. The very furniture and layout of a reference area can influence whether library users use the service that is offered. The stereotype of the dreary aloof reference librarian behind a high desk looking down on enquirers is potent precisely because it matches the secret fears (and, alas, experience in some cases) of library users. One should never forget the fact that asking a question involves a major vulnerability—the fear of being judged to be stupid. Another factor in approachability is simple presence. Is there always someone at the reference desk? How long does the library user have to wait before asking her question? How long is the line at the reference desk? How busy does the reference librarian appear to be when approached? How genuinely friendly is the response from the reference librarian? How good is the reference librarian at dealing with people of different ages, ethnicities, educational levels, and so on with the same level of courtesy and dignity? It is difficult, though by no means impossible, to use these and similar questions as part of the assessment of the reference service in your library. Another potent approach to evaluation is simply to put yourself in the place of the library user and ask, which characteristics would I like to see as a user of this reference service?

Being *knowledgeable* is obviously a minimal qualification for a reference librarian. (A good antidote to worries about "competition" for libraries from mega-bookstores is to think how rarely one encounters knowledgeability in the underpaid, untrained staff of those establishments.) The level of knowledge and the areas in which the librarian is knowledgeable are most important. A good reference librarian knows

> the collections (reference and general) in her library,
>
> the maps of the bibliographic universe provided by catalogues and classifications,
>
> the strengths and limitations of electronic resources available to the library's users,
>
> how to conduct a reference interview, and
>
> the nature and quantity of information that is appropriate to the person posing the reference question.

There are recurring patterns in research and reference behavior that are known to the expert reference librarian. They have been summarized by the estimable author and Library of Congress reference librarian Thomas Mann as:

- Patterns in the types of question that people ask, and in how they ask them
- Patterns in the usually unconscious assumptions they hold about what can be done
- Patterns in the bad advice they are sometimes given by teachers, employers, and colleagues
- Patterns in the mistakes and omissions that reduce the efficiency of their research[6]

Mann goes on to write, "Viewed collectively, these patterns tend to suggest the areas in which most people need the most help. . . ." Though Tom Mann lays out those patterns in a book aimed at helping individual researchers to be their own reference librarians, the patterns he describes play an important part in the reference interview and its outcomes. Skilled reference librarians take them into account and render their best service by complementing the problems they pose and giving the library users what they need, irrespective of how well those users have formulated those needs.

I wrote earlier that good reference librarians should be *comprehensible*. I am not referring only to their grasp of the English language, though here, as in all aspects of librarianship, the ability to communicate in clear, direct language is a decided asset. When considering the desired abilities in a reference librarian, knowledge at various levels is clearly very important, but it is also important to remember that knowledge can be negated by an inability to communicate it. A previously cited text provides a definitive brief explanation of communications in service: "Keeping customers informed in language they can understand and listening to them."[7] The important points here are the matter of using language that the reference service user can understand and the two-way nature of the communication. Just as the amount and type of information in a reference answer should be appropriate to the needs and nature of the questioner, so should the language used in answering.

A reference librarian, particularly one in a large general library, is going to encounter all kinds and conditions of people. The library in which I work is used daily by thousands of students, faculty, and community members. Many of the students are first-generation university students who are graduates of high schools with the worst school libraries in the United States.[8] A substantial number have a first language other than English. Many, possibly most, come from a disadvantaged (that is, low-income) background. The community members who use the library range from professional researchers and retired professors to high school students seeking assistance in writing papers. The faculty are highly educated and come from a wide variety of disciplines. You will see that it is necessary for reference librarians serving such a diverse population to be able to communicate at a variety of different levels and to recognize the appropriate level to communicate in each reference encounter.

Zeithaml refers to the need to listen in the service encounter. All experienced reference librarians know that the initial question rarely contains all that the questioner wishes to know. Most commonly, the first question is couched in much more general terms than the person really intends. For example, the question may be "Where can I find census data?" when the intention is to discover the number of Native Americans in California. Another example is "Where are your books on economics?" when the intention would be better conveyed by "I am writing a term paper on the deficits of the 1980s and would like some relevant information." Discerning the intention behind the question requires careful listening and probing—skills that the most knowledgeable may not always possess instinctively.

My colleague Dave Tyckoson is the author of the most important general article on reference of the decade.[9] In it he reviews the various alternatives to "traditional" reference desk services that have been proposed in the past fifteen years and finds each of them wanting. Those alternatives include expert systems (the use of technology as a substitute for human contact); interaction by electronic mail; "tiered" service in which different levels of staff categorize questions and deal with them accordingly; team staffing of reference desks; replacing immediate access to reference librarians by "appointment" systems; and eliminating reference service altogether. Tyckoson dissects each of these solutions and finds them wanting, the last coming in for some justifiably harsh criticism involving, as it does, drivel about "access engineers," "knowledge cartography," and the former reference librarian as market researcher.[10] His conclusion is that the only thing that is wrong with reference service carried out by means of the human-to-human reference encounter is that it is underfunded and undersupported. Reference librarians are under stress but that stress is not inherent to the reference encounter. It is caused by overwork and doing more with less. Library administrators who wish to work in libraries that function at a high level of service need to fund and support this most visible of all library services.

Comforting the Afflicted

A service philosophy should be promoted that affords equal access to information for all in the academic community with no discrimination on the basis of race, values, gender, sexual orientation, cultural or ethnic background, physical or learning disability, economic status, religious beliefs, or views.[11]

Perhaps the most obvious manifestation of the altruistic service ethic that pervades librarianship is our historic mission to help everybody, but especially the poor, societally disadvantaged, and powerless. In all kinds of libraries, you can see a concentration on service to those who need it most.

Knowing the Library User

It is an axiom in business that, in order to succeed, a company must have a customer base and provide services that base wants and needs. For that reason, most companies not only do expensive research into groups to which they wish to sell a product or service, but also pay large sums to maintain the information in that database in order to keep the information current. It seems easy to define the community served by any given library—a municipality; a university community; a company; a nation; pupils in a school; patients, nurses, and doctors in a hospital, and so on—but that ease of definition is often illusory. Almost all libraries also serve people who are outside their "natural" constituencies and that phenomenon increases as libraries cooperate and create more and larger alliances. However complicated it may be, the definition of the community served is essential if the library is to focus its services where they are needed. It is also important to define a core community and peripheral communities in order to apply budgeting and service priorities to each.

Public Libraries

The community served by a public library is defined by political boundaries and is funded on the basis of service to those who live in the political entity. Except in the case of small homogenous towns and sparsely populated rural counties, a public library will serve a wide range of people and differing groups defined by age, income, ethnicity, language, and so on. This is complicated further because, in addition to service to library users who live in the community served, modern public libraries have other users. Almost invariably, cities today are surrounded by separate political entities (suburban communities) that house large numbers of people who work in those cities and use their public libraries. Most public libraries are involved in cooperative arrangements that facilitate mutual acceptance of library cards from other public libraries, interlibrary loan, and other means for users of other libraries to use their services and resources. All the groups, within and without the political entity that funds the public library, have to be taken into account in formulating a service plan, including the priorities assigned to each group.

The heaviest users of public libraries are the young and poorer senior citizens—the least powerful groups in our society. As described in an earlier chapter, public libraries were created in the nineteenth century for the poor and, in many cases, evolved into "the people's universities"—the means for poor people to escape the bondage of poverty through self-education. In addition to the users in the library's buildings, public libraries have often reached out beyond their walls to provide services to the housebound and the incarcerated and to those in remote areas by means of mobile libraries. Bringing library services to the sick and the lonely and the desperate is another demonstration of higher levels of service. Almost all communities prize the children's library and its services above all other programs offered by the public library.[12] It is important in this context to note that children share with the poor and the old the characteristic of less mobility than other groups (the least mobile are poor children and poor old people). If service to children is a political and moral priority, the funding argument that rages in many places about local versus centralized public library service must be heavily weighted to local service.

Academic Libraries

Libraries that serve higher education at all levels—community colleges, liberal arts colleges, universities—almost always have a defined service community on which they concentrate. That community may be central but it does not include all those served by those academic libraries. To begin with, and especially for publicly supported institutions, there is also the population in the wider community—the "town." Colleges and universities, particularly large institutions in small towns ("college towns" like Urbana, Ill.; Bloomington, Ind.; and Ithaca, N.Y.), are a major cultural, political, and societal presence in their communities. They cannot, even if they wish, stand aside from the community and neither can the academic library. Publicly and privately supported institutions that hold depository collections of federal and state documents are obliged by law to make those collections available to any member of the public. Publicly supported institutions cannot deny access to their facilities to taxpayers and their families. They may withhold access to certain library services—borrowing privileges, interlibrary loan services, free copying—that they offer to their students and faculty, but they may not or cannot withhold other services.

On the most mundane, though important, level, we should note that few academic libraries are funded to provide, for example, reference services or access to electronic resources through terminals to persons who are not members of the academic community. Those users from outside that community cannot easily be persuaded that they are not entitled to the use of facilities and services that are largely paid for by the taxes they pay. Nor would it be in the political or moral interest of the academic library and its institution either to make that case or to act on it. To take a common example, many urban academic libraries are used heavily by high school students, particularly in the evenings and on weekends. There are numerous instances of reference librarians in those libraries reporting that they are inundated by requests for assistance from high school students, sometimes to the detriment of the service they give to "their" students. Similarly, many public terminals in those libraries are used in the evenings and on weekends by high school students trying to meet assignment deadlines. Not a penny of the library's funding is based on the provision of reference service to, or terminals for the use of, high school students. However, state universities and colleges that seek to recruit high-quality students have a particular interest in encouraging the kind of student who is diligent or intellectually curious enough to pursue an assignment in an academic library. On the one hand, the library is being asked to provide services for which it is not funded. On the other hand, the library is serving the educational goals of the high school students and the institution by providing those services. The answer, I believe, is a more imaginative approach to cooperation and funding for mutual benefit among all educational levels. Is there any reason *in principle* for opposing an integrated approach to funding library services for students from kindergarten through graduate school using state and local funding sources? Is there any reason *in principle* why public, school, and academic libraries in a community should not integrate their funding in search of maximizing the total library service for that community? The answer to both questions is no, but that does not explain away the enormous number of practical and bureaucratic obstacles to such a service-oriented approach.

Academic libraries spend a large and increasing amount of money on library instruction—a service that, by definition, disproportionately benefits disadvantaged students. The reason for the latter is very simple. There are three broad classes of entrants to state universities—high school graduates, community college transfers, and "re-entry" students. The high school graduates that need library instruction most are those from deprived backgrounds, because the method of financing public education means that the better schools are found in rich neighborhoods and the poorer schools in poor neighborhoods—the latter containing higher numbers of minority students. A high proportion of community college attendees are from the less-wealthy population (because of the far lower fees those colleges charge). "Re-entry" students are those adults who return to college, usually with the objective of improving their job prospects after they have been divorced or downsized or have undergone some other life-changing experience. Such library skills as they have are likely to be outmoded. All three groups add up to substantial numbers of people who really need library instruction to empower them to profit from higher education. I would suggest that one could not find a better expression of the service ethic than bringing familiarity with the world of recorded knowledge and information to those who really need it.

School Libraries

School librarians have a well-defined primary clientele—the children and young adults learning in the school the library serves. They have an important role in education, standing in the same relation to the school that the academic library does to the university or college. Their role is to provide another dimension complementing classroom instruction in giving access to recorded knowledge and information in all formats. They also have a strong instructional role—teaching young people how to use libraries and, even more important, helping in literacy teaching and the acquiring of a love of reading and learning. These heavy tasks require a variety of professional skills combined with dedication and empathy. The fact is that they are too often exercised in environments lacking necessary resources.

One of the sadder manifestations of the "crisis" in public education has been the decline of the school library in many states. When budget cuts hit, school administrators cut those functions that they regard as less essential. Given the hype about the Net and the Web, it is easy to see that such administrators, clutching electronic straws, class libraries (and the space they occupy—important to the distressing number of space-strapped schools) as "inessential" together with the arts, music, and other intangible benefits that are undervalued in a materialistic age. Far from being inessential, school libraries are vital to education, not least because they can be, and are, the basis for literacy and lifelong learning. Does anyone doubt that today's lower levels of young people's proficiency in reading and writing are linked to the underfunding of school libraries and their services? Even when schools maintained their "libraries" in the recessions of the 1980s and early 1990s, they often did away with their librarians. A "library" without professional assistance is just a room with books and terminals in it—not much of an advance on no library at all. (This is not to belittle the efforts of many nonlibrarians who fought mightily to keep the school library flame alive during dark times.) If we want strong public education—something that even its severest critics favor (at least nominally)—and believe it to be a mainstay of democracy, we must support and encourage strong school libraries and our colleagues who work in them.

Companies and Institutions

There are many, many for-profit and nonprofit concerns—from museums to research laboratories to software companies to foundations to law firms to auto manufacturers—that possess libraries. Those libraries are as various as the organizations they serve, and their services are tailored to particular clienteles. It is relatively simple for the librarians of those libraries to define their user groups and their mission. It is also relatively easy to gauge the success or otherwise of the service they offer. Because many special libraries are in for-profit entities and because their users are so clearly defined, it is not surprising that special libraries have been leaders in innovation in librarianship and the use of technology. This has benefited the profession as a whole as those innovations have often been transferable to libraries with more diffuse missions and user groups.

Other Kinds of Libraries

Some of the most rewarding and demanding jobs and opportunities to serve available to librarians are found in hospitals, hospices, retirement homes, and prisons. Without library values (particularly that of service), work in such libraries would be difficult if not impossible, and the difficulties of the users of those libraries would overwhelm the librarians who work in them. In some cases, the local public library is responsible for library service to the ill, the institutionalized, and the incarcerated. In many others, the library is part of the institution itself. Reading and other library services can be consolations and blessings to all of us; how much more are they consolations and blessings to those in extreme circumstances? Those who are ill or alone treasure reading matter that will take them out of themselves, that will provide insight into their condition and the human condition, and that will enable them to pass the days. Those who are imprisoned (more than two million souls in the United States today) read for those purposes, too, but they also read for more practical reasons—to learn the law and to become more educated. The rate of illiteracy in the prison population is far higher than among those outside, and increasing literacy is a proven antidote to recidivism. A prison librarian can turn a life around—an awesome responsibility but one that is in the best traditions of the service ethic of our profession.

Service—the Bottom Line

Libraries exist to serve their communities and society as a whole. Librarianship is suffused with the idea of service. It is very important that we continue to seek innovation in service, from any source we can. It is equally important that our service be informed with humanistic values as opposed to materialistic values. Business practices may well offer us some good ideas and approaches, but they should be used and adapted with caution. Our work is to serve the individual, groups of individuals, communities, and society, acting idealistically in a materialistic age. Those ideals, though, need to take reality into account—no one is served by impractical goals and visions divorced from reality.

NOTES

1. *Webster's Third New International Dictionary* (1976).

2. Barbara A. Gutek, *The Dynamics of Service* (San Francisco: Jossey-Bass, 1995).

3. Sharon L. Baker and F. Wilfrid Lancaster, *The Measurement and Evaluation of Library Services*, 2d ed. (Arlington, Va.: Information Resources Pr., 1991).

4. James L. Heskett et al., *Service Breakthroughs* (New York: Free Press, 1990), 2.

5. Valarie A. Zeithaml et al., *Delivering Quality Service* (New York: Free Press, 1990), 136.

6. Thomas Mann, *The Oxford Guide to Library Research* (New York: Oxford Unversity Pr., 1998), xvii–xviii.

7. Zeithaml, *Delivering Quality Service*, 22.

8. Since the Great Tax Revolt of the late 1970s, California's school libraries have consistently ranked fiftieth out of the fifty states by all important indices (pupil/librarian ratio, age of materials, etc.). See Michael Gorman, "The Domino Effect, or, Why Literacy Depends on All Libraries," *School Library Journal* (April 1995): 27–29.

9. David A. Tyckoson, "What's Right with Reference," *American Libraries* 30, no. 5 (May 1999): 57–63. The article is a sequel to Bill Miller, "What's Wrong with Reference," *American Libraries* 15, no. 5 (May 1984): 303–306, 321–322.

10. Jerry Campbell, "Shaking the Conceptual Foundations of Reference," *Reference Services Review* 20, no. 4 (winter 1992): 29–36.

11. Association of College and Research Libraries, "Intellectual Freedom Principles of Academic Libraries" (June 1999). *www.ala.org/acrl/principles.html*

12. *Buildings, Books, and Bytes,* issued by the Benton Foundation (Washington, D.C.: 1996), reports that children's services were by far the most valued library service in the focus group they assembled. See *Library Trends* 46, no. 1 (summer 1997): 178–223.

6

Intellectual Freedom

What Is the Meaning of Intellectual Freedom?

The phrase "intellectual freedom" is widely used to describe the state of affairs in which each human being has the freedom to think, say, write, and promulgate any idea or belief. In the United States, that freedom is constitutionally protected by the First Amendment to the Constitution, which states, in part, "Congress shall make no law respecting an establishment of religion or prohibiting the free exercise thereof; or abridging the freedom of speech, or of the press." There is, of course, no such thing as an absolute freedom outside the pages of fiction and utopian writings, and, for that reason, intellectual freedom is constrained by law in every jurisdiction. Here the initial and simple concept becomes tricky because, of course, there are just laws and unjust laws and, to put it simply, times and opinions change. Over the centuries, laws have banned certain kinds of political, social, sexual, literary, and religious expression. To complicate matters, some of those laws have been at the national level, some at the state level, and some at the local level, and have often been at variance each with the other. Over the centuries, one or more of blasphemy, sedition, and obscenity has been the target of government restriction. It seems that, today in the United States, only sexual expression deemed to be "obscene" is banned by law and, theoretically at least, all political, literary, social, and religious expression is free of government restraint. It does not help that "obscenity" has never been defined clearly and, hence, has been ruled to be a matter of local mores and values so that something that circulates freely in Greenwich Village may be forbidden in a small rural California community.

What Is the Relation between Intellectual Freedom and Libraries?

The complex of approaches to the question of intellectual freedom and libraries is spelled out in the article on the topic in the *Encyclopedia of Library and Information Science*.[1] It is noteworthy that the American Library Association has never defined intellectual freedom, particularly given the existence of ALA's Office of Intellectual Freedom (reason, in and of itself, to be a member of ALA) and given the fact that ALA has made many statements and taken many positions on many aspects of the topic. From the ALA point of view, intellectual freedom begins with opposition to censorship of books and other library materials—hence the activities and publications centered on the annual Banned Books Week. From there the topic expands to include ALA's stand on the library user's right to gain access to all library materials, which, in turn, is connected to the librarian's duty to make all library materials available to everyone. The librarian not only has a duty to library users but also has rights that are personal to her or him. Those rights include, but are not limited to, freedom of expression, the democratic process in the workplace, and the right to pursue any chosen lifestyle. Related to all this is the concept of the library as an advocate of intellectual freedom. That notion is not without elements of controversy, because it sets up the clash between those who believe in advocacy and those who think that the library should be neutral in all social conflicts—including those that relate to the First Amendment.

It can readily be seen that intellectual freedom begins as a question of a basic and, to many, inalienable human right opposed in principle only by those who do not believe in social equality and democracy, but soon leaves that relatively simple field of argument. The fact is that many quarrels about intellectual freedom are not between those who are for it and those who are against it. They are often between people who believe in different applications of intellectual freedom, while all professing to be for it. There are those who are "absolutists" and would deny no one the right to create, disseminate, say, see, or read anything at all. There are those who agree broadly with that notion, but would restrict access to certain materials by certain groups—for example, children. There are also those who use the "protection of children" as a stalking horse for their comprehensive censoring agenda. Therefore, in considering intellectual freedom issues, we should always be aware that we are not dealing with good and evil—though both may well be present—but with a complexity of views, many of which are sincerely held. After all, the debate over "protecting" children from the Net is about what is best for children. Some may believe that the intellectual development that comes from free access to all recorded knowledge and information is worth the risks. Others wish to shelter their children from unpleasant reality. Yet others wish to restrict the reading and viewing habits of all children, including those for which they have no direct responsibility.

Librarians believe in intellectual freedom because it is as natural to us, and as necessary to us, as the air that we breathe. Censorship is anathema to us because it inhibits our role in life—to make the recorded knowledge and information of humankind freely available to everyone, regardless of faith or the lack of it, ethnicity, gender, age, or any other of the categories that divide us one from the other. I strongly believe we should hold fast to intellectual freedom and carry out our tasks without reference to our own opinions or the opinions of those who want to restrict free access to knowledge. I should acknowledge that, as an academic librarian, I am comparatively better off than fellow librarians in other areas. After all, academic librarians work in an institution that is overwhelmingly dedicated to the idea of academic freedom; we tend to work for people who share that ethic; and we are usually not professionally isolated. Compare that context to the lonely battles that are fought by librarians in small, rural public libraries and by solitary school librarians battling obscurantist school boards. If you look at the lists of challenged and banned books that are issued each year, you will see that those are the people in the front lines. All the more reason to support our library associations' offices of intellectual freedom in the great work they do on our behalf to protect this most important professional value.

Intellectual Freedom in Action

Most library associations and related professional bodies have a statement on intellectual freedom that exhorts their members to apply the concept of intellectual freedom in all the activities of the library. One of the best of these is the Canadian Library Association's statement of June 27, 1974 (amended November 17, 1983, and November 18, 1985).[2] It reads (in part):

> Libraries have a basic responsibility for the development and maintenance of intellectual freedom.
>
> It is the responsibility of libraries to guarantee and facilitate access to all expressions of knowledge and intellectual activity, including those which

[*sic*] some elements of society may consider to be unconventional, unpopular, or unacceptable. To this end, libraries shall acquire and make available the widest variety of materials.

It is the responsibility of libraries to guarantee the right of free expression by making available all the library's public facilities and services to all individuals and groups who need them.

Libraries should resist all efforts to limit the exercise of these responsibilities while recognizing the right of criticism by individuals and groups.

I have pointed out previously that intellectual freedom is a complex matter with many dimensions. In practical application in libraries, the use of even the CLA's innocent seeming admonitions can and do create problems. There are no problems for the absolutist and the censor, of course. The first would allow everybody to have access to everything. The latter would choose what is made available and to whom, based entirely on individual preferences and convictions. For the rest of us, the world is infinitely more complex and one to be negotiated in the light of both principle and practicalities. Here are some real cases:

> A school board orders two novels on contemporary Latino life to be withdrawn from a class reading list and limits their availability in the school library.

> A public library board is taken over by an organized group of "social conservatives," which orders filtering software to be installed on all library public terminals used to give access to the Net and the Web for both adults and children.

> A group of citizens calls for a nineteenth-century work of literature to be withdrawn from the library because of race-insensitive terminology.

> A religious group donates copies of its publications and then cries "censorship" when they are deemed outside the scope of the collection and not added to the shelves.

> An anarchist group wants to meet monthly in a public meeting room in the library and display publications calling for armed opposition to the government.

Then, suppose that your work life, job, and even career may depend on how you deal with these issues. This is the point at which one might well see a clash of values. There is the value of intellectual freedom in the first instance, but there is also the value of service to a community. You will notice that most of these real-life examples occurred in small towns, school districts, and public library systems. A person who genuinely believes (and with good reason) that she is personally important to the health of library services in a small community may well feel inclined to make small accommodations to the forces pressing on her in order to preserve the greater good of the library and its users. If you are inclined to decry those small accommodations, please weigh your own circumstances against those of the librarian in question. Please also consider the value of taking a stand against the value of a useful, productive career. Let us also consider this practical question: If the librarian in these cases stands on her principles and is fired, whom do you think the people who fired her will hire? Do you think it would be another First Amendment absolutist? I will yield to no one in my admiration for those who take the moral high ground and I would never advocate a spineless truckling to power, but I do want to make the following fundamental points. Life is never as uncomplicated as it appears from a distance. Small sacrifices may well, on occasion, benefit the majority of library users. One does not have to be perfect to be able to live with one's conscience.

Fighting the Evils of the Web

The American Library Association has been waging the just war against censorship for many decades. It has stood, as we have seen, for freedom of access to recorded knowledge and information for everyone, without regard to their age, gender, ethnicity, religion, or any other distinguishing characteristic. Many of the battles fought by ALA and its members center on the relatively simple (and constitutionally protected) issues of the freedom of the press. It says it right there in the First Amendment, and, though some can and do argue that there should be limits on what you can print and read, the overall issue is very clear to most Americans, and, if only in the long run, the good guys usually win. If only the Founding Fathers had the prescience to include "freedom of the Web"!

When you think of all the battles waged over freedom of the press, banned books, and censorship in the Print Age, it is difficult to believe that we may come to look back nostalgically on that time because of the appalling complexities introduced by digital resources of all kinds. In 1998, 40 percent of American households contained personal computers. A substantial number of those computers are linked to the Net and the Web and those numbers are increasing inexorably. Schoolrooms and public libraries contain computer terminals more or less as a matter of course. Use of the Net is only surpassed by hype about the Net. It is hardly surprising, therefore, that those who favor censorship in general are much exercised about the Net and the Web and advocate measures to prevent unlimited access to those resources, particularly by children and young adults. It is difficult, when the media winds blow so hard, to step back and have some historical insight, but it is well worth doing. Almost every new means of communication in the past century and a half has been greeted as being, *in itself*, an assault on the morals of the nation, particularly the young. (I write "almost" because I cannot recall newspaper stories about microfilms rotting young minds.) Just think of the havoc that silent movies wrought on the flappers; the awful toll on the morals of young, unmarried people dancing to gramophone records; and the modern evils of "gangsta" rap and movies that drive children to homicidal mania. Why, there was even a popular book in the 1950s that denounced the corrosive effect of the "hidden messages" contained in comic books.[3] Violent movies are not new, but the Net and the Web are, and librarians have to deal with hyped-up attacks on them and those who give access to them. "Children have always looked for forbidden books, magazines, and other media, and guardians of public morals have often blamed such sources for a decline in juvenile behavior."[4]

Let us face an important fact. When censors and filterers talk about "culture" and "moral decay," they mean the dreadful duo—sex and violence. Those, too, are nuanced. To some people, any depiction of, or writing about, sex is offensive. To others, it is only images and writing about sexual variations that offends. Then there is the John Wayne Problem—which, stated succinctly, is: If violent images are harmful, why is the violence in *The Green Berets* acceptable? Because Wayne was a good actor in a "patriotic" film? Surely, the example of violence toward others in a "just cause" is as harmful as the violence of a video game. If it is not, then the often advanced "cause and effect" argument is confounded or, at least, shown as the unbearable complexity it is.

Every "threat" posed by a new means of communication has been met by calls for legislation to make the world, especially children, safe from the perceived iniquity. In 1999, the ALA Intellectual Freedom Committee reported that there had been a number of legislative proposals (some enacted) at the federal, state, and local levels to defend children from the Net and the Web.[5] Each of these proposals contained the same flaws (in the words of the report). They

> fail to define what constitutes "harmful to minors,"
>
> require librarians to police minors' use of the Internet,

disregard the fact that children and minors have First Amendment rights, and

intend to block constitutionally protected speech for minors, as well as potentially block that speech for adults.

They also mandate the use of filters in public terminals in public libraries— devices as ineffective as they are philosophically offensive (see the discussion later in this chapter).

Before going on to discuss filters as such, let us see what they are designed to achieve. The central concern of those who genuinely wish to protect children (as opposed to lifelong censors who are using the Internet as the latest weapon to achieve their social aims) is that children may see or read images and texts that are morally harmful. It is very easy to find stuff on the Web, advertently or inadvertently, that is aesthetically repulsive, inherently sordid, or exploitative of humans. None of those constitutes an offense to morality— unless, that is, you believe that your own morality is or should be universal. The latter is only acceptable to those who use statements beginning "The American people believe . . . ," thinking that they are equipped to decide what the majority of this vast, diverse nation believes on every issue. I do not eat meat. Pictures of factory farms and of meat being cooked are repulsive to me. Does that mean that I should do everything in my power to stop others (who may or may not eat meat) from seeing those pictures? That may seem absurd, but is it really any more absurd than me seeking to stop people from seeing pictures of people engaged in sexual variations that do not appeal to me?

Then there is the question of the assumed superiority of those who would censor. The idea is that such people can read texts or view images that will have no effect on them but will be "harmful" to other, presumably more suggestible, people. Someone once defined a censor as someone who does not want you to know what he knows. Could it be that the effects of texts and images on the individual psyche are simply incalculable—as unpredictable as any other effect on individual behavior? Anyone who is honest with herself will acknowledge that some sexual or violent images and texts stay in the mind for years and exercise power over that mind. These are images and texts that have been ignored or forgotten in minutes by millions of viewers and readers but, for some reason, hold sway in one mind for a lifetime. It is difficult for me to believe that violent or sexual images on the Internet do much good to anyone, but it is equally difficult to imagine that they do much harm either. Millions of people around the world have watched the horrific violence of the *Rambo* and

Die Hard movies, but the worst that happened to 99.999 percent of them was wasted time.

Japanese popular culture is saturated with vividly violent and searingly sexual images and texts—manifest, among other places, in Japanese Web sites. Japan's level of violence is lower by many magnitudes than the level of violence in the United States. Further, there is no evidence at all that sexual mores in Japan are inferior to those in the United States. What does that tell us? First, that Japanese society and culture are very different from the society and culture of the United States. However, it also tells us that exposure to violent and sexual images and texts is not a determining factor for the nature of a society. Denmark and the Netherlands are well known for their permissive attitudes toward, among other things, sexual writings and images. Is there anyone who would seriously argue that Danes and the Dutch are morally inferior, as a whole, to American people? Well, yes—those who think that sexual writings and images are inherently wrong. In other words, the argument has turned in on itself and we are no longer discussing the "harm" that is alleged to be done, but the imposition of one morality on those who may or may not share it.

Children

ALA has rendered itself unpopular with a vocal minority by stating a constitutional fact—children and young adults share the First Amendment rights of those over age eighteen. (One would have thought this might be obvious in states in which people can marry at age sixteen or younger.) Even if you believe that viewing and reading can harm those under eighteen, you still have to come to terms with the necessity of abridging those rights in order to prevent that "harm." That being so, it seems to me that it is important to define that harm and gauge its extent. There have been thousands of studies of the effects of television watching on children. (Television watching and Internet surfing are very similar activities, though the latter seems different because of its potential for interactivity—despite the fact that most surfing is as passive as television viewing—and because it is the newer, "hotter" medium.) Many of the studies reinforce the obvious—that spending many hours a day watching programs with little intellectual content and social value is not good for the minds and bodies of children. Some seek to show that watching programs with sexual or violent content can do psychological harm. The evidence for the latter is much less conclusive. Many researchers believe that there is no direct and strong correlation between acts of violence and watching acts of violence on television and that television programs are a minor part of a web of social factors that lead to antisocial behavior by some children. "On balance, it seems likely that any relationship that may exist between watching television violence and perpetrating actual violence is likely to be a complex one, and a number of contributing factors must be considered."[6]

If the connection between violence on television and the Internet and violence in life is difficult to discern, how much more difficult is it to define the connection between sex on television and . . . what? Most children are intensely interested in sex and seem to have a natural ability to cope with the level of truth about sex that is appropriate to their age. Many sexual writings found on the Net and many sexual images and situations seen on television and the Net are tawdry and unedifying. What else is new? Most portrayals of anything on television and the Net are tawdry and unedifying. No, the objection to children having access to sexual materials through modern media is the same as the decades-old objection to sexual content in books, films, and other material. It is rooted in a morality and an ideology that wishes to protect the "innocence" of children from the "corruption" of sex. It is the duty and obligation of parents to guide and advise their children in their reading and viewing habits, and they, and they alone, should police those habits in the light of their own morality and convictions. I would much rather young people were reading *The Joy of Sex* than watching slasher movies or playing violent video games, but that is my morality and I would not seek to ban either on the basis of it.

Filter Fever

The most commonly proposed remedy to protect the young from the perceived and actual ills of the Net is called "filtering." Filtering programs purport to screen out "undesirable" sites. Filtering advocates are those who wish to make those undesirable sites unavailable. They are opposed by those who claim that filtering is an unconstitutional infringement on the liberty of the individual. With all due respect, I would maintain that this age-old clash over a new issue is completely irrelevant. The truth is that filtering systems *do not work* and they *never will work!* They do not work because they are based on the same keyword searching using an uncontrolled vocabulary that gives you 48,332 "relevant hits" on the simplest Net search. Any librarian with knowledge of bibliographic control knows that controlled vocabularies and close classification are the *only* way to ensure precision and comprehensive recall. The mirror image is that the only way to have filtering systems that work would be to catalogue and classify fully every Web page! ALA is on record as opposing filtering (principally on First Amendment rather than practical grounds) and has, therefore, drawn the ire of would-be cyber censors: "by advocating open access to hard-core smut . . . [ALA] has constructed a protected haven to corrupt our innocent."[7]

The Strange Case of "Dr. Laura"

Welcome to the world of "Dr. Laura" [Schlessinger], a leading figure in the social atavism movement. Unlike many of the mail order "Reverends" and "Doctors" who infest that movement, she actually has a respectable, if marginally relevant, academic background.[8] She is the purveyor of a highly rated (as of July 1999, second only to Rush Limbaugh) right-wing radio show and a successful writer of books and newspaper columns. Her aim in life is "a total make-over of society."[9] In hot pursuit of that aim, her Savanarolian eye fell on the American Library Association in the spring of 1999. The *casus belli* was a link from the ALA Young Adult Division's Web page to another Web site called Go Ask Alice run by those well-known pornographers, Columbia University. Go Ask Alice gives straightforward advice about social, sexual, spiritual, and emotional health. What interested "Dr. Laura" was, of course, the sexual element. It turns out that, if you really dig for it, you can find advice on various sexual variations in Go Ask Alice. Who knows whether "Dr. Laura" believes that teenagers should not have an interest in sex and its complexities or, perhaps, believes that those sexual complexities should not exist or, perhaps, was avidly in search of some more hot stuff to feed the insatiable radio and newspaper audience? However it may be, she went to battle ALA and its advocacy of access "to hard-core smut"—that is, its principled rejection of filtering software. It turned out that the link in question begins with the "Health and Medicine" section of a Web site called Teen Hoopla constructed and recommended by the Young Adult Division of ALA (YALSA). It was, therefore, an electronic equivalent of an entry in a "reader's guide" leaflet of the old days. The trap, of course, is that once you enter the Web by a link of any kind, you are staring at the endlessly receding mirrors of a fun house.

> Despite the enormous size of the Web—it now has some 800 million pages— enough pages contain multiple hyperlinks that it is possible to get anywhere on the Web by traversing only a few links, according to a paper in today's issue of the journal *Nature*.[10]

To put it in its starkest terms, if a group of dedicated professionals trying to serve the wider public (at their own time and expense, it should be noted) cannot recommend a site created by other professionals at Columbia University, librarians cannot make *any* links from their Web sites. If "Dr. Laura" had her way, we would take our cumulated experience and guidance right up to the edge of electronic resources but no farther. ALA has overreacted to criticism from "Dr. Laura" and is reviewing its policy on Web links. It is feared that this means that ALA may override the judgment of its members and, thus, precipitate an unprecedented struggle over values. The saddest thing of all is that any such action would be pointless, because, if it were designed to turn away the wrath of the likes of "Dr. Laura," it will never work. I seldom agree with journalist and perennial presidential candidate Patrick J. Buchanan, but he is correct in saying that there is a "culture war" (a direct translation of *Kulturkampf*, a Nazi-era term) being waged in this country. Attacks on the likes of Go Ask Alice are tactical maneuvers in that war (of which the discussion of filtering is a major battle) and the proximate cause of that attack is merely a symbol. The "Dr. Laura" minicrisis (she caters to the attention span of her audience by finding new targets with great frequency and moved on quickly from ALA "peddling smut") is really about her wish, and the wish of those who agree with her, to censor, and the mission of ALA and librarians in general is to provide the most access to the most people.

Combating Filter Fever

I do believe that ALA has been less than effective in its opposition to filters but it is not easy to deal with what is, fundamentally, an irrational proposal. Rather than fighting this battle on philosophical and moral grounds—from which we will always emerge theoretical victors and actual losers—I believe that librarians should have a two-pronged strategy. First, it is essential to make the point about the inutility of filters. It is certainly not difficult to demonstrate that blocking by keywords does not work. Most Web users understand that keyword searching is ineffective—regular encounters with thousands of marginally relevant (at best) "hits" using search engines have annoyed enough people for long enough. All we need to do is to demonstrate the reason why such events happen (the use of keyword full-text searching) and then to make the connection with exactly the same technique used in filters. Second, we need to put out a more positive message about the use and limitations of the Web and the Net, the need for parental involvement in the use of libraries by minors, and the need for minors to read more books.

The last thing we need to do is to squander the accumulated capital of goodwill that libraries and librarians have built up over the years—particularly not in a fight in which librarians can be portrayed as the enemies of morality and as ivory tower purists eager to sacrifice children and families (not to mention our colleagues in many small libraries) on the First Amendment altar. The opponents of intellectual freedom managed to demonize the American Civil Liberties Union in the 1970s and 1980s, partly by misrepresenting that excellent organization's beliefs and activities. Does anyone believe that the same number could not be done on ALA if we persist in laying ourselves open to misrepresentation?

This is no war of shadows without consequences, nor is it a war between good (ALA) and evil (the filterati). ALA does act from good motives and is philosophically, morally, and intellectually on the right side. The filter fans may be led by demagogues and bullies, but they include many people holding sincere religious convictions and with serious concerns about the culture and the future of their children. Those people can be reached and should be the targets of our arguments about the filter fallacy, the need for parents to participate in library use, and the uses and value of literacy. We should also have a good deal of sympathy for our colleagues in the kinds of communities in which the filter wars are being fought. Many of them simply cannot understand why those of us in different circumstances appear not to know about the pressures that are being applied. For example, the city council in Nampa, Idaho, voted to withhold $50,000 in acquisitions funds from their public library materials budget (of $120,000) unless the library installs filters on its Internet terminals.[11] The librarian of the Nampa public library was still in the process of considering the filter issues and was clearly being pressured by this attack on her book budget. She joins a large number of our colleagues who are not only in danger of losing their jobs but also of seeing the libraries that they have worked so hard to build being gutted. The bizarre ideological confusion that surrounds filtering is nowhere better illustrated than in the Nampa case. According to *Ljdigital,* this action is the latest in a series of attacks on the library that began with complaints about the library owning *Heather Has Two Mommies* and *Daddy's Roommate* and refusing to move them to the adult section.[12] The fact is that this and other filtering arguments are clearly just the latest front in the censorship wars that have been going on for decades. Despite this, we must never forget that filtering is a powerful symbolic representation of the real fears of many people who are not particularly ideological. On their behalf and on the behalf of colleagues caught in the filtering cross fire, we, as a profession, must devise an effective and successful strategy to counter filtering.

That strategy will do the following:

Stress the positive contributions that librarians and libraries make to society.

Make reasonable accommodations to concerned parents.

Demonstrate the ineffectiveness of filtering.

Stress the importance of reading.

Stress the constitutional underpinnings of the First Amendment rights of children and adults.

Stress the parental duties to guide, advise, and monitor the reading and viewing habits of children.

Use all available public relations and marketing techniques to get these messages to the widest possible public.

We should use advertising and all other means of mass communication to build on the generally favorable view that the public has of libraries and librarians. We have a good story to tell and have earned the respect and esteem of the public. We will add to that respect and esteem if we manage to persuade the majority of parents that we are reasonable by such actions as requiring permission in writing for children to use public terminals connected to the Internet and placing those terminals used by children in plain view. I have discussed the ineffectiveness of filtering and would add here that we should make that case as forcefully as possible. We need to place great emphasis on the importance of sustained reading to intellectual development and fight against the Internet hype. A child reading a good book is the positive answer to the fears to which filtering and the V-chip are negative answers. We should never yield our belief that children have rights, too, and that those rights include the right to free enquiry. Surely we could find common cause with most concerned parents in stressing the preeminent role of parents as guides and mentors. None of this will persuade "Dr. Laura" and her ilk, but it will reach the sensible mass of people as a counter to their propaganda. If it is a propaganda war, then let us fight it as such. For example, a professionally produced video from ALA making all the points listed here would be a potent aid to public and school librarians in their discussions with all but the most obscurantist school and library boards.

Libraries and censors have been around for centuries. The grounds change, the causes change, media of communication change, but the idea of liberty of thought and expression is the same as it was in the age of Tom Paine.

NOTES

1. *Encyclopedia of Library and Information Science,* ed. Allen Kent (New York: Dekker, 1974).

2. *The ALA World Encyclopedia of Library and Information Services,* ed. Robert Wedgeworth (Chicago: ALA, 1980), 442.

3. Frederic Wertham, *The Seduction of the Innocent* (New York: Rinehart, 1954).

4. George Dessart, "Barring *Rambo* from the Potemkin Village: Reflections on the V-Chip," *Television Quarterly* 28, no. 3 (summer 1996): 37–41.

5. "ALA IFC Report to Council, Tuesday, June 30 [1999]," *Intellectual Freedom Action News* (June/July/August 1999): 6–10.

6. Kirstin J. Hough and Philip K. Erwin, "Children's Attitudes toward Violence on Television," *Journal of Psychology* 131, no. 4 (July 1997): 411–416.

7. Laura Schlessinger, Letter to ALA Executive Director, William Gordon, May 5, 1999.

8. A Ph.D. in physiology from Columbia University.

9. Patrizia Dilucchio writing in the online magazine *Salon.com.*

10. Vincent Kiernan, "As Goes Kevin Bacon, So Goes the Internet, Researchers Report," *Chronicles of Higher Education* (September 9, 1999), *http://chronicle.com/free/99/09/99090901t.htm*

11. *Ljdigital* (April 30, 1999), *www.bookwire.com/ljdigital/leadnews.article$29049*

12. These two books have been attacked because they portray children in households headed by lesbians and gay men.

7

Rationalism

What Is the Meaning of Rationalism?

Rationalism is simple to explain. It is the practice of guiding one's opinions and actions by what is considered reasonable. The philosophical belief that reason is a source of knowledge in itself—independent of emotions, faith, and the senses—is the basis for the rational approach. Like most values, it is not an absolute. Paradoxically, a total reliance on reason is quite unreasonable, and one should always be wary of those Gradgrinds who exalt reason above everything and lose their humanity in the process.[1] However, in the practical matters of the world, a tilt toward reason over emotion is always to be preferred.

Rationalism under Attack?

There seems to be a great tide of fundamentalism, superstition, and plain craziness in the world today. From faith healers to militants of all stripes, the world is full of people who are convinced that they know the One True Way and are aggressively intolerant of those who do not share or, worse, laugh at, their irrationalism. It sometimes appears that the classical conflicts of most of the twentieth century—left versus right, North versus South, capitalism versus communism, white versus nonwhite—are fading into the mists of history. They are being replaced by a broad single conflict between the forces of internationalism and secular rationalism and what one writer describes as "atavistic social movements" that oppose both.[2] This is not to espouse the notion proposing that the triumph of democratic capitalism over communism means that we have reached "the end of history."[3] Rather, I wish to place the various forms of irrationalism in a global context. Nor would I state, most simply because I do not believe it, that internationalism and particularly its manifestation known as "globalization" are preferable to their alternatives in all instances. Insofar as they mitigate the many evils that nationalism and fundamentalism (of all kinds) have visited upon the world and its inhabitants, surely we can argue that movements that bring people together are to be preferred to movements that set one type of person against other types. Further, surely we can argue that rational, logical, and humanistic beliefs have proven to be more beneficial than irrational and antihumanitarian beliefs. I would stress here that I do not use "rational" as the opposite of "spiritual" but as an antonym of "irrational."[4] It is perfectly possible for a person to be both rational and spiritual, and reason and rationality are not the foes of faith.

It seems to me that libraries are children of the Enlightenment and of rationalism. They stand, above all, for the notion that human beings are improved by the acquisition of knowledge and information and that no bar should be placed in their way. We stand for the individual human being pursuing whatever avenues of enquiry she or he wishes. We also stand for rationalism as the basis for all of our policies and procedures in libraries. Bibliographic control, collection development, reference work, library instruction, and so on are all based on rational approaches and the scientific method. Librarianship is a supremely rational profession and should resist the forces of irrationalism both external and internal.

What Is the Relation between Rationalism and Libraries?

As far as libraries are concerned, rationalism is important in two different ways. First, all the practical aspects of librarianship—what older writers used to call "library economy"—benefit from the application of reason. Cataloguing, reference work, library instruction, collection development, materials processing—all must be guided by policies that are firmly based on the rational method. Second, there is no better antidote to the forces of unreason than a well-stocked, well-organized library—the natural home of someone seeking objective information and well-founded knowledge and with the willingness to discriminate between them and the ill founded and the unreasonable. I wish to examine three aspects of library work in the light of rationalism. I chose them because they exemplify rationalism in a way that other aspects of librarianship that are predominantly influenced by personal interaction (reference work, etc.) do not. The three are:

- the ways in which we organize libraries
- library instruction as a rational process primarily aimed at imparting the rational approach
- bibliographic control as the ultimate expression of the rational approach

Organizing Libraries

One important application of rationalism and belief in reason in libraries is, or should be, the way in which we organize libraries in order to carry out our mission. Too often, organizational structures have grown by accretion—like coral reefs—in which the original, long-forgotten organization has been shaped and added to for different reasons at different times. Why does one library have three technical services divisions when another library of similar size and mission has one? One will get you ten that the three departments were created around long-gone personnel issues or to respond to long-solved issues and problems. The other problem with long-established organizational patterns is the Old-Shoe Syndrome. Most people are more comfortable staying with the familiar than working with new people in new work patterns. If one has the power and is determined to apply the rational method, shouldn't such accidental organizations surely be swept away and replaced with more efficient structures? Surprisingly often, the answer to that question is no. Rationalism calls for a clear appraisal of the practical effects of each policy and procedure and it might be that an organization that has grown unplanned would, on examination, prove to be working quite well. Accepting a productive organization that may appear to be illogical is a very rational thing to do. On the other hand, we should not accept ineffective organizational structures because they are familiar and comfortable. Sensible change may, on occasion, have bad effects on morale in the short term but yield increased morale in the longer term, because effective organizations make people more productive, and most people are happier when engaged in productive work than when they feel their work is ineffective or even futile. Probably the best weapon the rational reorganizer has is that most rational of all maxims, Occam's Razor:

Entities should not be multiplied without necessity.[5] In other words, a library should have the smallest number of departments and other organizational units, the smallest number of steps in the hierarchy, and the smallest number of staff in each unit that is consistent with effectiveness.

Let us try to adduce some principles of organization derived from rational analysis of work in libraries and the functions that units within libraries are designed to perform. I would propose the following:

> The ideal organization should be as "flat" as possible. That is, it should have the least number of steps in the hierarchy that is consonant with the library's mission.
>
> No one should have an impractical number of people reporting to her or him. The late Hugh Atkinson used to invoke the minyan as a model for the upper limit of the number of people reporting directly to an administrator, though even that number seems high to me.[6]
>
> Organization of work should follow my "drift down" theory of library organization, which states, aphoristically, that no librarian should do what a library technician can do, no library technician should do what a clerical staff member or student assistant can do, and no human being should do what a machine can do.[7]
>
> The units of the library should have a clear mission and explicitly defined and demarcated responsibilities.
>
> Each unit should be staffed with enough and no more than enough people at appropriate levels.
>
> No organizational unit should be based on either personalities or temporary exigencies.
>
> The organizational structure should be flexible enough to allow for the formation of temporary groupings (task forces, etc.) to deal with specific projects and temporary challenges.
>
> Units concerned with the general functions of the library should be organized around those general functions (collection development, reference, cataloguing, etc.) and not around types of material. The exception to this tenet is the case of materials that either need machines to be useful (microforms, sound recordings, etc.) or need special handling, storage, and conservation (manuscripts, archives, etc.).

All organizations should permit and encourage cross-training leading to flexible deployment of human resources.

Organizations should permit and encourage individual advancement.

It is soon apparent that, in practice, some of these prescriptions may conflict.
For instance, it is difficult to create and maintain a "flat" organization and an
organization in which no one has a lot of people reporting to her or him. The
flattest organization, after all, is one in which everybody reports to one person. This is illustrative of the central problem of organization, which is that
theory and practice can conflict—and usually do. Another manifestation of
that problem is that most administrators have to deal with existing structures
and work patterns and seldom have the luxury of sweeping change or, luxury
of luxuries, the chance to build a new organization from scratch. That practical realization does not mean that administrators have to abandon the rational approach any more than the rational approach means that all libraries
must, willy-nilly, be forced into impractical, theory-based structures. As with
so many philosophies and values, rationalism is an approach, not a prescrip-
tion, and the successful administrator is one who achieves balance between
theory and practice, between pragmatism and ideals.

Teaching the Rational Approach

Information versus Instruction

One of the more controversial duties of the librarian is the duty to instruct.
Melvil Dewey stressed the teaching role of librarians.[8] Others have called that
role a fiction.[9] From the earliest days of public libraries, in which the role of
the librarian as elevator of the cultural level of the community was taken for
granted by most, to the most modern wired library of today, there has been
considerable discussion and debate about whether it is proper for librarians to
see themselves as teachers. Public librarians have largely abandoned that idea,
but school librarians in most states are teachers in name as well as fact. The
history of librarians teaching in academic libraries is relatively recent but
complex and difficult to untangle. It revolves about the central question of
whether it is better to deliver the recorded knowledge and information that a
user wants and needs or to teach that user to find what she needs herself. The
mock-Oriental cliché about the superiority of teaching people to fish rather
than giving them fish has been invoked often. This seemingly sage remark
does not, of course, take into account the person who just wants a fish to satisfy

his immediate and temporary hunger and, consequently, resents the time-consuming process of learning how to fish. It is difficult to imagine a less service-oriented approach than that of denying a simple request for help in the interest of educating the requester in a skill that she may never need again.

Why Bibliographic Instruction Developed

Teaching about libraries used to be called "bibliographic instruction" (BI) in academic libraries. BI has a long and interesting history arising in great part from two phenomena of thirty to forty years ago:

1. the movement that established undergraduate libraries on major college campuses in the 1950s and 1960s[10]
2. the manifold deficiencies of bibliographic control in the age of the mammoth card catalogue and successive layers of unsatisfactory cataloguing rules

The first phenomenon segregated undergraduate library users in designated places physically apart from the "main" or "graduate" library. (This latter was by no means an unintended consequence for the senior faculty who encouraged the undergraduate library movement.) It also created a subspecialty within academic librarianship of librarians devoted to the special needs of undergraduate students. This contrasts with smaller university libraries and college libraries, in which reference service, collection development, and bibliographic control are directed to the full range of library users from freshmen to internationally renowned scholars.

Card catalogues become virtually unusable at a yet undiscovered size (it will never now be defined, as these behemoths are all dead or dying). Many millions of volumes arranged by the LC or Dewey Decimal classification are, to put it mildly, difficult to navigate. Printed indexes to periodical literature are, at best, slow and tedious to use and, worse, months if not years out of date. These negative factors defined the environment in which a student was supposed to do library research in research libraries before the advent, O blessed day, of the online catalogue and the electronic index. It is hardly surprising, therefore, that the relatively new specialty—undergraduate librarianship—should focus on programs that were dedicated to help undergraduates find their way through the shockingly unfriendly bibliographic maze that lay outside the more user-oriented confines of the undergraduate library. Bibliographic instruction, in short, sought to make up for the many and manifest inadequacies of bibliographic control in large academic libraries until the early to middle 1980s.

BI did evolve from that simple aim, however. It sought to become a new branch of librarianship in itself. Its more avid adherents seemed almost happy to deny easily bestowable help to the library user in need in favor of making that user jump through some BI hoops. They were accused of seeing BI as a subject in itself rather than a tool to help library users and of ignoring the real needs of library users. BI was even accused of being a cloaked attempt to raise the image and status of academic librarians by equating them with teachers. (Remember that this was a time in which the arguments about "faculty status" for librarians raged unchecked.)

Why BI Was Transformed

Time may not have been a great healer in this instance, but it was certainly a great transformer. As online catalogues and periodical indexes and abstracting services became more sophisticated and easier to use, the need for "bibliographic instruction" became less and less. The introduction of rationality to bibliographic standards (MARC, ISBD, AACR2, etc.), their widespread adoption, and the consequently high level of second-generation online catalogues and union databases made instruction that was specifically "bibliographic" less important to library users. The result was that BI was reborn as "library instruction"—programs devoted to teaching people how to use the library and find what they need. In other words, the emphasis swung from the negative (making up for the deficiencies of rotten systems) to the positive (how to make the most of the library and its services). These LI programs were, in turn, transformed by the widespread availability of electronic resources in libraries, either through the Net and the Web or from databases that the library maintains or to which it subscribes. Given the seductive power of electronic resources and the ease with which one can find "something" on the Net, it is hard to argue that library users do not require some instruction aimed at understanding the value and severe limitations of electronic resources. In fact, in academic libraries, that need is so manifest and universal that it has, for the time being at least, settled the old "information versus instruction" debate. Today's student needs both help and instruction, and both in great quantities.

"Library Instruction" and Public Libraries

Before I go on to discuss the application of rationalism to instruction in libraries, I wish to touch on the question of "library instruction" and the lack of it in public libraries. Schools and institutions of higher learning have, in varying degrees, captive audiences. Leading university librarian Hugh Atkinson once said, "An ounce of help is worth a ton of instruction." It is hard to argue that it is practical to deny public library users their ounces of help when they are simply not available to receive their ton of instruction. Formal programs of library instruction are inappropriate in almost all public library settings, so the discussion tends to revolve around using reference work not only to answer the questions of the moment but also to inculcate the best way to find desired information in the future. Roma Harris's research indicated that (at least in Canada ten years ago) there was a very high level of agreement among public librarians that reference work should involve an element of instruction, even when it was not requested by the patron.[11] It would stand to reason that the massive influx of electronic resources into public libraries in the 1990s would have, if anything, strengthened that agreement. Everyone from the federal government to Bill Gates says that every public library should be wired for the "information age," beginning, in Gates's case, with the poorest areas of the country. Poor areas are inhabited disproportionately by those with less education than most. Given those circumstances, it is almost impossible to think that people should not be taught how best to use the inordinately expensive resources created by wiring the nation's public libraries. Call it what you will, "library instruction" is not just for colleges anymore.

Rationalism and Teaching the Library and Its Resources

Once a library of whatever type has accepted the need for instruction in use of the library and its resources (which I will continue to call "library instruction" for want of a better, more inclusive term), it must formulate and understand the rationale for such a program. Given the fact that the human resources available are likely to be limited (some of the already overburdened reference librarians in all probability), it is vital that the program be focused on the most pressing needs. In most libraries, the most obvious need is for instruction and assistance in the use of the Internet and other electronic resources. It is likely, however, that one problem in the use of the Internet is that it blinds the uninformed to other sources of knowledge and information that are available in the library. A primary skill crying out for instruction is the choice of the most appropriate and effective sources (print, electronic, etc.) to fit individual questions and problems. Many people need to be taught that no one type of resource can supply the answers to everything. In an age of commercialism and hype about the Web and the Net, that is not an easy point to make. Devising a rationale for an instruction program depends, in the first instance, on defining the skills that are most important to the library's users.

"Library instruction" is a slightly old-fashioned term now. People use "information competence" as if it were a substitute or development of library instruction, but, on examination, it turns out not to be so. All the information competence programs that I have seen are concentrated entirely, or greatly, on electronic resources and the search for digital information. They are, therefore, based on the idea that the virtual library is an emerging reality and that recorded knowledge of the kind found in print is no longer relevant to the concerns of library users. Far from seeing information competence as a progression from library instruction, I see the two as complementary and, indeed, in need of augmentation. I have become convinced that the teaching that goes on in libraries will have to encompass basic computer skills, in the short term at least. I think it is entirely possible that, as computers become more widely available, they will become easier to use. For the time being, however, many people, particularly the poor and otherwise disadvantaged, need help and instruction on what is now deemed to be a basic tool. Given that, I believe that rational thinking about instruction in libraries leads inevitably to programs that combine computer competence, information competence, and library instruction.

The instruction program of the future, whether carried out by formal instructional means or integrated with reference service, should have three ascending components:

1. basic library and computer skills
2. how to identify, locate, and use appropriate sources
3. critical thinking

These three components each deal with the use of "traditional" library materials and electronic resources. Please note that I am talking about both formal instructional programs that are typical of academic and college libraries and indirect instructional programs that are planned parts of reference service in public libraries.

At the first level, students will learn about libraries—what they are and what they contain. This may seem to be self-evident but, to a person unused to public library use and with only scant, involuntary involvement with a school library that had no librarian to advise and teach, elementary facts about libraries can come as a revelation. This level of instruction would also contain introductory facts about computers to enable the technologically challenged to be at ease in computer use and, thereby, able to use electronic resources to their advantage. This last may be the one opportunity for public libraries to attract large numbers of their users to formal classes.

At the second level, library users will become aware of the bibliographic structure of the library and the ways in which we organize recorded knowledge and information for retrieval. At this stage, it is vital that instruction should differentiate among the three concentric rings of organization:

1. the highly organized and structured environment of the library, featuring authority control, controlled vocabularies, bibliographic standards, the artificial language of classification, and so on

2. the less-organized environment of journal indexes, abstracting services, and the like, featuring a lack of standardization between different indexing entities but vocabulary and name control within a particular service

3. the disorganized environment of the Net and the Web, in which the user has to rely on random aggregations of sites (such as those found in Yahoo! and other popular services) and search engines based on keyword searching

At each level, both *relevance* (the match between the search terms and the documents retrieved) and *recall* (the percentage of relevant documents retrieved) are degraded. In other words, one of the most important lessons that must be taught is that the same search using the same terms will yield very different results in different environments. This matters a lot because a search that yielded a few highly relevant documents in a catalogue or index will, in all probability, yield a large number of mostly irrelevant documents on the Net. In the latter case, the temptation for the uninitiated is to take whatever is found without even knowing that there are far more relevant documents among the large number retrieved. The instruction here should be dedicated to ensuring that library users cannot just locate *something* but can locate and identify the materials that are most relevant to their needs. Those materials will sometimes be books, sometimes journal articles, sometimes other media, and sometimes electronic documents. The strategies that must be imparted are dedicated to distinguishing the strengths and weaknesses of each medium and the various paths by which the most relevant of them can be located.

The third level is that of critical thinking. The ability to distinguish the true from the false, the relevant from the irrelevant, the wise from the meretricious, and the shallow from the deep has always been a part of enlightened education. It is probably fair to say that, until the advent of the Internet, librarians were happy to leave such instruction to school and college teachers. After all, we all knew which publishers were reputable, which newspapers and journalists were authoritative, and which journals ranked highest in their fields. A librarian had obviously done her job well in giving a direction to a library catalogue or indexing service that led a user to a book published by Oxford University Press or Random House, an article in the *New York Times* or *US News and World Report*, or an article in the *Journal of the American Medical Association* or *Nature*. Today, all bets are off. Just telling someone to look something up on the Internet can scarcely be accounted a job well done. The various medical sites that are proliferating on the Web may or may not contain relevant and accurate information. A search on Alta Vista that yields 4,932 hits cries out for an alternative (another search or another source). It is clearly impossible for a librarian to be there to help each library user lost in the wasteland in which, for example, the *Washington Post* and the *Drudge Report* are on equal footing. That being so, librarians must do their best to ensure that the user's struggle with the Net and the Web is not a completely unequal contest. The equalizer in that struggle is critical thinking—the ability to evaluate and judge documents in all forms and from all sources.

The rational approach to librarianship demands that we dispense instruction and, in so doing, enable library users to be empowered by knowledge and relevant information.

Bibliographic Control

Apart from their physical plant, libraries have three assets—their collections (tangible and intangible), their staff, and the architecture of bibliographic control. Good buildings, collections, and staff without bibliographic control are glorified mega-bookstores. A collection with bibliographic control but no staff is a glorified warehouse. The best staff and the best organization in the world cannot make up for inadequate collections. A Russian riddle asks, "Which is the most important leg on a three-legged stool?" thus emphasizing the interdependence of the three pillars of a good library. Collection development and the hiring and care of staff have more of art than science about them, but bibliographic control is the epitome of rationalism and the "scientific approach" in librarianship.

Standards

The modern age of librarianship began in the late 1960s and culminated about ten years later. In some respects, that golden age provided us with the foundations of libraries for the next century. The breakthrough events that characterized that period were the spread of library automation and the concurrent and linked spread of effective and accepted bibliographic standards. MARC—the globally accepted standard for electronic bibliographic records—was born in the age of the card catalogue and is present today as an essential element of the most advanced Web-based library system. The *Anglo-American Cataloguing Rules, Second Edition* (AACR2) made national and international standardization of the content of MARC records possible and achievable, not least because it incorporated the International Standard Bibliographic Description (ISBD) global standards. AACR2 is now the de jure or de facto standard in all English-speaking countries and in many that are not. It is also the basis for many codes written in other languages. We have national standards for classification (the Dewey Decimal and Library of Congress systems) and subject headings (the LC *List of Subject Headings*—LCSH), but they are not as widely accepted internationally.

The point of this near-global bibliographic standardization is not that cataloguing has improved (though it almost certainly has) but that it has made some longtime dreams realizable. Librarians have been building union catalogues and aspiring to a universal union catalogue since the middle of the nineteenth century. Two things made those goals impractical until thirty years ago—the technology of the time and lack of standardization. It is impossible to create and maintain a *current* union card catalogue, book catalogue, or microform catalogue. Until 1979, not even Britain and North America shared a common cataloguing code, still less the rest of the world. Computer technology and standardization made massive current union catalogues possible and even made the dream of Universal Bibliographic Control (UBC) achievable.[12] UBC is a program that states, in essence, that we should use technology and standards to ensure that each document is catalogued once in its country of origin and the resulting record is made available to libraries and researchers throughout the world. Viewed in this light, the various international and national cooperative cataloguing schemes of the Library of Congress and the gigantic world union catalogue that OCLC has created represent a harmonic convergence of rationality and dreams. We have come to a point at which the rational approach typified by cataloguing, standardization, MARC, and cooperation will enable the creation of a seemingly fantastic dream—the World Catalogue!

What about Electronic Documents?

It would be a great irony if, on the verge of achieving the World Catalogue, we were to use it solely for access to tangible documents (books, maps, journals, etc.). It is imperative that we ensure that this universal bibliographic resource includes records for, and links to, worthwhile electronic resources. The rub lies in those last few words. What is worthwhile? Which electronic resources? I have written of the value of stewardship and the consequence of deciding what is or is not significant in chapter 4 of this book, and now wish to apply that criterion to electronic resources and their peculiar problems.

To simplify, there are two basic problems with electronic resources as far as bibliographic control is concerned. The first is that the majority of such electronic documents or aggregations of data are of no value, little value, very localized value, or temporary value. The second is that electronic documents are inherently unstable and shape-shifting. These two simple points add up to a massive complexity that may, at first, seem to defy rational analysis and a rational set of answers. It is clearly neither rational nor efficient to catalogue a mass of electronic documents that are valueless or of limited value. It is clearly not efficient to catalogue something that may have a completely different shape and content in the future. It might be natural to despair and hope that, left alone, the great swamp of electronic records will somehow resolve itself. I think such a course of action would violate the two important values of stewardship and rationalism and believe there is another, much more difficult and expensive, plan for the future.

One part of that plan would be to blend traditional cataloguing and "archival" cataloguing. By the latter, I mean the cataloguing of aggregations of documents rather than the documents themselves. Some electronic documents will be of sufficient importance to be catalogued on their own; others (including but not limited to Web sites) should be catalogued in groups with their individual components listed briefly, if at all.

Another much-discussed issue is that of "metadata"—a pompous word meaning "data about data," which, when you come to think about it, applies to any form of cataloguing. The most popular manifestation of metadata is "the Dublin Core," an ill-defined subset of the MARC format that deals with the structure (a rather skeletal structure) of the bibliographic record and hardly at all with its content.[13] In a way, metadata is a panicky response to the perceived immensity of the problem and a solution from the "anything is better than nothing" school of thought. The point is that, in considering the cataloguing (by whatever name) of electronic resources, we do not need new structures and new standards (and certainly not those as ill articulated as the Dublin Core). It is possible to catalogue *any* document in *any* format using AACR2, a major classification, the LC subject heading list, and MARC.[14] The question is not *how* to catalogue electronic documents but *which* electronic documents to catalogue. My proposal is to devise a system in which electronic documents would be evaluated in terms of their value and whether that value is general and permanent (as opposed to local and temporary) and, thereby, sorted into the following categories:

1. those to be catalogued fully, using all bibliographic standards
2. those to be catalogued using an agreed, enriched version of the Dublin Core
3. those to be catalogued using the skeletal Dublin Core
4. those to be left to the mercies of search engines and keyword searching[15]

These categories are in descending order of permanence and value. They are in ascending order of number of documents in each category. The first category would comprise no more than 2 percent of electronic resources (though even that seems a high estimate of the proportion of permanently valuable items). The second and third categories might add up to another 10 percent, and all the rest would be dealt with as they are today. Those percentages are pure guesses, of course, but even if they are roughly correct, foretell a massive and sustained cooperative cataloguing effort over many years.

If all the political, strategic, and financial questions were answered and this grand plan were to be implemented, libraries would still be faced with the fragile nature of electronic documents and the need to preserve those that had been catalogued. Such electronic preservation schemes as have been proposed lack credibility. Those who care at all about preservation (as all librarians should) are either fatalistic or optimistic that some technological solution as yet undreamed of will show up. Even if it does, what about the documents of today, which may well be lost by the time the Great Solution appears? The fact is, there is only one certain way to preserve electronic texts and images and to ensure their transmission to future generations. That is to print them on acid-free paper, make many copies, and distribute those copies to a number of libraries. When you have eliminated the implausible, whatever remains, however low-tech, must be taken seriously!

NOTES

1. Charles Dickens, *Hard Times* (1854).

2. Meredith Tax, "World Culture War," *The Nation* (May 17, 1999): 24.

3. Francis Fukuyama, *The End of History and the Last Man* (New York: Free Pr., 1992).

4. "Not according to reason; unreasonable," in *Webster's New Collegiate Dictionary* (1960), s.v. "irrational."

5. William of Ockeghem (1285–1349) is best remembered for Occam's Razor, which states, "Entia non sunt multiplicanda sine necessitate."

6. "A quorum or number necessary for conducting Jewish public worship—15 by the rules of *Mishnah,* not less than 10 . . . ," *Webster's Third International Dictionary of the English Language* (1976), s.v. "minyan."

7. Michael Gorman, "A Good Heart and an Organized Mind," in *Library Leadership: Visualizing the Future,* ed. Donald E. Riggs (Phoenix: Oryx, 1982), 73–83.

8. "The time is when the library is a school and the librarian in the highest sense a teacher." Melvil Dewey, "The Profession," *American Library Journal* 1, no. 1 (September 30, 1876): 5–6.

9. Pauline Wilson, "Librarians as Teachers: An Organizational Fiction," *Library Quarterly* 49 (1979): 146–152.

10. The first undergraduate library was established at Harvard University in 1949. *www.fas. harvard.edu/~lamont/history.shtml*

11. Roma M. Harris, "Bibliographic Instruction in Public Libraries: A Question of Philosophy," *RQ* (fall 1989): 92–98.

12. Franz Georg Kaltwasser, "Universal Bibliographic Control," *UNESCO Library Bulletin* 25 (September 1971): 252–259.

13. See Michael Gorman, "Metadata or Cataloguing?: A False Choice," *Journal of Internet Cataloguing* 2, no. 1 (1999): 5–22.

14. LCSH is often and rightly criticized as to its content (the actual words used to denote subjects) but not for its structure. In other words, subject headings can be changed and new headings added to that structure.

15. See Gorman, "Metadata or Cataloguing?"

8

Literacy
and Learning

In these days, when more of us run than read, and when what we know exceeds what we understand, let me urge a return to the book. The book remains that small handy instrument that we call a key. We can all carry it and with it we can unlock most of the doors to the unimaginable beauties that lie somewhere beyond the TV set, to the east of the movies, and to the west of the moonshine that flows from too many media of communication. Best of all, the book is not a fleeting fancy. It is steady. It remains ready for reference, for reassurance, and paradoxically for the comfort of companionship as well as the luxury of solitude. I am for it.[1]

What Is the Meaning
of Literacy and Learning?

Read: v. To take in the sense of, as of language, by interpreting the characters with which it was expressed ... To learn or be informed of by perusal

Peruse: v. To read carefully or critically ...

Literate: adj. Instructed in letters; able to read and write ... n. One who can read or write ...[2]

These are suspiciously simple definitions. It is obvious that deciphering a child's ABC book is a very different activity than reading at a high level, yet we call them both "reading." It may be significant that another dictionary adds the description *archaic* to the word "peruse," as if reading carefully and critically were such a rare activity that a word describing it is no longer necessary. The matter of reading is both complicated and critical to the future of the life of the mind, and we cannot understand libraries or human learning unless we place literacy in context and explore its meaning thoroughly.

Learning to Be Literate

In the common course of human development, a child will learn to speak and then learn to see more than random squiggles when presented with letters or characters. She will then learn that those letters or characters are capable of being linked in words, phrases, sentences, paragraphs, chapters, and, ultimately, complete texts. This process, which is usually accompanied by improvements and extensions in speech and vocabulary, can be described as "learning to decode." It is the necessary precursor of understanding (though, of course, the dawning of understanding often accompanies the process of learning to decode). If you think of the process of learning a foreign language after childhood, you will see that, in learning, say, French or Spanish, you have a knowledge of most of the characters, and very little else. Even if the words assembled from those characters look vaguely familiar, you probably have little idea of how to pronounce them or what they really mean. So the process of learning a foreign language is a process of proceeding from the basic characters through decoding to understanding, in the same way as acquiring the ability to read one's native language. It is a long road from

> The cat sat on the mat

to

> Where the shadow is regarded as so intimately bound up with life of the man that its loss entails debility or death, it is natural to expect that its diminution should be regarded with solicitude and apprehension, as betokening a corresponding decrease in the vital energy of its owner.

This sentence from Sir James Frazer's *Golden Bough* not only contains some words not commonly found in everyday speech, but also expresses a complex thought that requires analysis and understanding. Also, it is but one sentence in a mammoth twelve-volume exposition of a complicated and multidimensional subject. A person needs more than the ability to read in order to read that book with intellectual profit. She needs the basic decoding skill but, beyond that, the ability to interpret, think critically, understand, and learn.

According to David Wood, a shift in learning occurs typically between the ages of eleven and thirteen.[3] At that time, it appears that students begin to learn more and absorb more from the written word than they do from speech and observation (this effect is true regardless of the level of reading ability). This observation reinforces the central importance of being able to perform sustained reading and use that activity to learn. It is interesting in this context to observe that the great majority of people learn more from and retain more of the knowledge contained in lectures if they take notes. In other words, it is important to be able to read even an abbreviated version of a spoken communication in order to reinforce that mouth to ear to brain experience by a supplementary eye to brain experience! In the same passage, Wood also emphasizes the importance of advanced reading to speech and the ability to achieve true literacy (his words apply to schoolchildren but surely have force for all of us of whatever age):

> The child who is fortunate enough to achieve fluent levels of literacy has at her disposal a whole new range of words, linguistic structures, and skills in planning which [sic] enable her to create interesting, informative, dramatic, and *coherent* [his emphasis] narratives . . . she has command over a range of literary devices and structures that can be exploited in speech to make what she says dramatic, flexible, variable, versatile, and, should she so wish, fast and efficient.[4]

Thus, literacy is not just a question of reading and writing, even at the highest level, but also an ability to express oneself fully. Some see the three abilities (reading, writing, and speech) as inextricably intertwined. I think that reading is the central portion of this complex in that one *could* live the life of the mind in isolation with printed texts—not the most highly recommended way of life but certainly possible—whereas, it is safe to say, writing well is impossible for someone who does not read, and expression through speech may be vivid but will lack depth and substance unless it is accompanied by sustained reading. (Some might dispute these assertions with reference to preliterate and illiterate societies and the oral tradition. Though I can see the force of their argument, I would counter with these facts. What we know of, say, *The Odyssey* and *Beowulf* come from the written record. For good or ill, we live in a time and society in which the oral tradition is not in any way central to the culture and life of most people, except in the bastardized and malign form of entertainment television.)

Broadly speaking, human beings learn in three ways:

They learn from experience.

They learn from others (teachers, gurus, guides) who are more knowledgeable and learned than they in at least one area of human knowledge.

They learn by interacting with the records of humankind found in books and other tangible and intangible documents created by other human beings.

From the very beginning of humankind, we have learned from experience. Humans and their predecessors learned what was good to eat and what bad from experience, and in the same way they learned to interpret weather signs, where to seek shelter, and all the other essential skills of survival. There were teachers before the invention of tools, of making pictures, and of writing—in those distant times, older humans (parents and family) taught the younger ones about life and survival. The third way of learning—by study of the records of humankind—became possible only when writing and drawing were invented. Those innovations abolished space and time, both of which severely constrain learning from experience and learning by interaction with a teacher. The records of humankind (whether carved on stone, printed in a book, or contained in an electronic file) consist of words, images, and symbols. To profit from those records, one needs to be skilled in understanding words and symbols and interpreting images. When skilled, we are able to interact with the minds of long-dead men and women and, adding a miracle to the miracle of the onward transmission of human knowledge, create new knowledge and record that knowledge for those yet unborn.

Reading, an activity that is routine to most of us, is in truth miraculous and should be cherished and encouraged. We speak of "learning" and "literacy" as if they were separate ideas, but they are inextricably linked. Literacy is more than a means to learning—although it is one of the most important means. In a real sense, literacy is learning and the sustained reading of complex texts as necessary to the developed mind as are air, water, and food to the healthy body. Reading at a level above the practical is a way of developing the mind, and the interpretation of texts is a rewarding intellectual activity in itself.

How Literate Are We?

There is a general idea that literacy rates have been climbing over the decades and centuries and that our society today is more literate than any of its predecessors. This fits with the "onward and upward" view of human history that, in essence, equates advances in technology with advances in culture and the health of society. Also, the presumption is that more than a century of mass education must have produced a literate society. A check in the catalogue of any large library will reveal masses of titles over many decades on the question of literacy and society that betray an unease about where we are and where we are going. We can see a lack of satisfaction with the state of literacy and learning from the famously anxiety-producing *Why Johnny Can't Read*,[5] through Neil Postman's 1985 book on "amusing ourselves to death,"[6] to any of the books of the late 1990s on literacy in a digital age. Why is this so? The simple answer lies in what one means by "literacy." If the word means the ability to read at some level, then we have mass literacy (even though about 5 million American adults are actually illiterate and 18 million American adults have reading ages below nine years).[7] If, however, to be literate means the ability to read and interpret complex texts (sustained reading) *and* the habit of doing so regularly, then the United States consists of two nations (not divided by class, race, or economics, in this case). The first nation contains the majority of people who can read enough to be able to function in society and in their work but seldom read other than for uninstructive recreation or out of necessity. The second nation contains a minority that reads to learn and elevate their consciousness. Alan Purves calls the latter "scribes"—people who can not only code and decode text, but also have a rich basis of reference that enables them to understand and create complex texts.[8] In his estimation, "the ratio of readers and non-readers is probably the lowest ever in American life since the time of the Massachusetts Bay Colony." (This last quotation demonstrates one of his points—in order to be truly literate, one needs not only to be able to read and understand the words in a text but to share in the scribal nexus of knowledge that enables the reader to realize the meaning behind the decoded words—in this case, knowing that the Colony existed in the seventeenth century and was made up of people fleeing religious discrimination, and that dissenters of that time were avid readers of the Bible and religious texts.) Another analysis finds three groups: a well-informed "reading elite"; a large and growing group of people who can read but rely mostly on television and other media for information and entertainment; and an underclass of the illiterate and uninformed.[9]

Two big questions arise if we come to believe that we live in a society that is made up of two (or three) nations—the aliterate/illiterate and the truly literate. They are:

Has anything changed?

What are the consequences for society and for individuals?

It is tempting to see our present situation as simply a contemporary version of the societies of the past. There have always been elites and masses, the learned and the ignorant, the educated and the uneducated. The civilization of Ancient Greece, from which comes almost all that is good about modern civilization (democracy, the rule of law, education, philosophy, and on and on), was based on a small proportion of educated, prosperous people supported by a large number of uneducated slaves and serfs. More than a hundred years ago, Oscar Wilde wrote that twentieth-century technology would make possible a Utopia—a re-creation of classical Greece with machines replacing helots and all citizens able to enjoy the fruits of the world and the pleasures of the intellect.[10] Wilde got it right about the technology (just look at modern agriculture, which combines unparalleled productivity with a small number of human farmworkers), but was obviously wrong about society. At the end of the twentieth century, almost everybody in the developed world had unprecedented levels of material prosperity and freedom from drudgery, but can we really say that the general level of culture had increased? The forces that dominate society—television, mass marketing, advertising, the commercial-entertainment complex—seem to be more powerful than the drive to learn and live the life of the mind for the majority of people.

So, are we worse off than we were fifty, one hundred, two hundred years ago? Are we better off? Perhaps neither is the case and only the details of society change. Optimists would point to the large number of books and magazines that are published each year. Pessimists would invite you to look at the *New York Times* list of best-sellers, dominated as it is by self-help manuals, shopping and romance novels, ghostwritten biographies of television nonentities and sports people, and hyped-up drivel tied to movie deals. Optimists would point to "the promise of the Internet." Pessimists would suggest you look at the content of the Net—porn and violence, paranoid ravings, gossip "journalism," stultifying personal trivia, enormous accretions of transient and local information, and the odd golden nugget too often obscured by the mountain of dross. Optimists would point to the high percentage of people who *can* read and write. Pessimists would point to the relatively small percentage who *do* read and write at anything beyond a functional level. Such an argument is almost endless, as are the facts that can be adduced to support either side. What does not seem to be in dispute is that the understanding and power over one's life that come from literacy and its exercise are of great benefit to the individual, both materially and psychically. Those who deal with the world by reading and writing in order to understand are better off in almost every way than those who do not.

What Are the Consequences of Two Nations on Either Side of the Literacy Divide?

This is a most important question for all of us because the health of society depends on there being a balance of interest between the elites and the mass of people. The former may well be the driving force in society, empowered by their knowledge to dictate, or, at least, heavily influence, the lives of others and the ways in which society is developing and changing. However, in the words of John Oxenham,

> To those who hold democratic values, it is also important that the majorities of people should have an adequate understanding of what the minorities [the elites] are up to and be able to exercise some intelligent and informed control over them. Already it is arguable that even very literate citizens in relatively democratic polities find themselves unable to maintain a satisfactory grasp of the workings of their societies.[11]

Notice that the power elites overlap with the literate elites but are not identical. In other words, there are a number of truly literate citizens who have little control over the politics and economics of society. How do we ensure that everybody in a society has, at least, the chance of being as knowledgeable and informed as those in power? Literacy and the ability to deal with the torrents of information are, surely, essential prerequisites.

What Is the Relation between Literacy and Learning and Libraries?

Despite the definitions at the beginning of this chapter, we have seen that literacy is not a simple question of being able to read or being unable to read. Literacy is best seen not as a state of being but as a process by which, once able to read, an individual becomes more and more literate throughout life; more and more able to interact with complex texts and, thereby, to acquire knowledge and understanding. It is a key element in the enterprise—learning—to which all libraries are dedicated. Instead of accepting the world as permanently divided among the illiterate, aliterate, and literate, we should see literacy as a useful technology to end that state of affairs. Viewed thus, literacy becomes an open-ended range of possibilities in which librarians, educators, and students work together to learn and become more learned using sustained reading of texts as a central part of the life of the mind. In this respect, the distinctions between kinds of librarians become unimportant—a children's librarian or school librarian is as important to the early stages of literacy and learning as a public librarian or academic librarian is to the later stages. We are all involved in the same process—providing the materials, instruction, and assistance that enable individuals and societies to grow and to thrive intellectually. Incidentally, it is not a question that is of marginal importance to academic librarians. (I am not speaking here of the reading abilities or willingness to read of the average high school graduate—that is a separate matter of concern, though a manifestation of the direction society is taking.) Whether a librarian accepts the existence of two nations divided by literacy is not crucial to this discussion. The fact is that, whatever your view of the state of literacy today, literacy is important to individual well-being and societal achievement and a goal to be pursued by all libraries.

What Should We Do?

All librarians can and should be involved in promoting literacy to one extent or another. The most important thing that we can all do is to build and maintain collections of books and other texts that are as rich and rewarding as possible, considering the mission of the library and the resources available. We should also encourage reading and the love of the self-improvement and pleasure that reading can bring. In all but the most specialized libraries, some (maybe a large proportion) of the library's actual and potential users will not be interested in reading and will need encouragement to raise their levels of literacy. This means that it is no longer enough to build the collections and hope that they will come. Active steps to guide users to reading are called for, and the more methods (large and small) that the library employs the better. Simple things like new-book displays and new-book lists sent to library users by e-mail or available on a Web page can raise the consciousness of even the most educated users. Lectures, other public events, and publications can also be used to promote reading. Some kinds of libraries can create formal literacy programs using teachers, peer counselors, and advisers. Others may only be able to use more indirect means. Two things need to be emphasized, irrespective of the type of library. First, literacy programs, formal and informal, should not be limited to teaching the mechanics of literacy but should also aim at instilling the lifelong habit of reading. Second, all libraries are in the literacy game and should work together, formally and informally, to advance the cause, each in its own way.

School and Children's Libraries

I should begin this section by stating unequivocally that children are better off reading books and other texts than they are watching television or surfing the Net. I also believe that librarians dealing with children can do no better thing than promoting reading and the love of reading. Children can only benefit from electronic technology when they are firmly established as readers. School and public children's librarians can have a formal involvement in reading and writing classes for children. They can also provide an environment that encourages reading outside the classroom (for schoolwork or pleasure). Displays, talks, story times, and contests are all tested and effective ways of bringing literacy to children. The attractiveness of the collection is central to the success of these libraries, because it is difficult to persuade a child to abandon all the many distractions of modern life in favor of old and unattractive reading matter. The popular wisdom says that school and children's libraries should be wired to enable children to be in touch with the "information age." I believe this is a tragically mistaken policy that is likely to decrease literacy rather than advance it. There are those who would say, so what? (see the end of this chapter) but they are people who do not value reading. Unless strictly controlled, the seductive power of images and "surfing the Net" (recently shown to be an addiction that afflicts millions of Americans) will distract young minds from the relatively difficult but rewarding task of reading books into the vacuousness of pointing and clicking.

Public Libraries

Public librarians can play a direct role in adult literacy programs by using their libraries as tutoring centers as part of the program introduced by Senator Paul Simon's 1984 amendment to the Library Services and Construction Act (LSCA). We should note here that Senator Simon had specific reasons for designating libraries as teaching centers. He felt that not only were librarians people who appreciated the enriching powers of reading and writing more than any other group but also that libraries were places that adult illiterates could enter with neither shame nor embarrassment. One writer believes that the central feature of successful adult literacy programs in public libraries is the "institutionalization" of those programs—their complete integration into the mission, goals, and programs of the library.[12] That integration has, of course, great implications for the funding and planning of library operations and for the way in which the library presents itself to the community. In other words, the public library must become not just a convenient home for the adult literacy program but embrace that program as a natural part of what it does. The result is, of course, that a successful literacy program will ensure that the number of people who can take full advantage of the library's programs and collections is increased. Beyond that, in raising the level of literacy in the community, the library is, *and is seen as,* a valuable community asset. Thus, an integrated adult literacy program is good policy on both idealistic and pragmatic grounds.

Colleges and Universities

Academic librarians can encourage reading and writing through participation in Great Books and other, less formal, programs. They can also participate in the regrettably large numbers of "remedial" classes found in all but the most elite, selective institutions. The sad fact is that many students who are accepted into higher education today are the product of a society and a school system that has de-emphasized basic skills, including the most basic skills of all—reading and writing. I am not making a political statement here and am a strong supporter of public education and increased funding for public education. However, I also believe that K–12 education would be transformed for the better if it were based on a syllabus that sought, from the earliest ages, to give intensive instruction in literacy and numeracy based on classroom teaching, supplemented by reading and writing assignments and experiences. The emphasis on technology over reading and creativity over basic writing skills, not to mention the proliferation of new and peripheral subjects, has produced a generation of nonreaders and poor writers. In many states, notably Proposition 13–wracked California, school libraries have deteriorated to the point of collapse. Is it any wonder that this witches' brew has resulted in the need for remedial education in colleges aimed at bringing students up to competence levels at which they can deal with university-level courses? I have come to believe that the evolving structure of "library instruction" (see chapter 7) not only must accommodate basic computer skills but also should be coordinated with remedial English classes to raise the levels of literacy among incoming students. This is a very different idea of the role of an academic librarian, and one on which many may frown, but altered circumstances call for new solutions and actions.

Special Libraries

Two years ago, the state of California, for the first time in its history, spent more on incarcerating people than on educating people. There is neither the space nor the need here to discuss the reasons for this troubling fact or the fact that the United States incarcerates more of its people per capita than any other nation on earth. Suffice it to say that there is a huge and growing population in prison—a population that is disproportionately illiterate and semiliterate. This is not the only negative indicator about the incarcerated, but it is among the most telling. The scourge of illiteracy is the ultimate powerlessness of those deprived of liberty and is the antithesis of the freedom and power of the educated and literate elite. If rehabilitation is still an aim of imprisonment, literacy education is a key element. I admire many of my librarian colleagues but, as a class, I admire prison librarians more than most. Prison librarians can act directly to attack illiteracy and to encourage those in prison not only to better themselves but also to find in reading the antidote to the despair of the lower depths of society. Prison librarians can use the range of methods to combat illiteracy, from the provision of reading matter to actual classes and tutoring in reading and writing. This again is another manifestation of the combination of idealism and pragmatism in the best of librarianship. Not only is it good to open mental doors for those with little help, it is also very practical—what are the chances of an illiterate former convict getting a job on release from prison?

Many special librarians have only the most general involvement with the question of literacy and have little chance to advance reading and writing specifically. However, as we have seen in the case of prison librarians, that is not always the case. For example, librarians in hospitals, particularly mental health facilities, can and do advance reading as a source of pleasure and diversion and, quite often, as an element in the healing and rehabilitation process.

Is There an Alternative to Literacy?

At the beginning of the twenty-first century, the question of reading and writing texts is still central to culture and communication. There are those who believe that technology will supply (and is already supplying) at least the possibility of alternatives to reading and writing texts that will enable people to become both educated and fulfilled in a postliterate society. Anyone attending meetings on university campuses will be familiar with chatter about "paradigm shifts" in learning and the importance of other "literacies"—"visual literacy," "computer literacy," and so on. All such talk is an attempt to deal with two facts.

> Most university students write at a level that is inferior to their counterparts of two or three decades ago and, by no coincidence at all, read less and read less well than those counterparts.

> At the end of the day, all educated people have to deal with texts, whether in the form of print on paper or from a computer (in more than 95 percent of cases, also printed on paper), and, if they cannot read books effectively, will be unable to read texts that emanate from computers.

These are stubborn and contradictory realities. There are only two real answers—bringing students back to sustained reading (against the grain of their pre-university education) or evasion. Examples of the latter abound and usually center on either the substitution of graphic or visual "information" for text or the birth of "new worlds" and "new ways of thinking" based on cyberspace or virtual reality or both.[13] The prose that encases such proposals is so opaque as to be virtually unreadable. Of course, clear, concise, declarative language is hardly to be expected from authors who are attempting to express in written words an alternative to written words as a means of learning and growing. In a paper that advances, I think, the idea that computers will make possible new visual means of storing and imparting knowledge that are superior to text, Pamela McCorduck writes:

> [Text] . . . will be joined by other epistemologies or ways of knowing and high among them will be a return to visual knowledge. But, I suspect, for that way of knowing to be as effective as text, knowledge must be encoded in a way that will demand the same level of attentiveness that text now does.[14]

Well, quite. I have read her paper with a suitable level of attentiveness and find no proposal that addresses the problem of encoding knowledge visually in a more intense way than we have for centuries of drawing, painting, photographing, filming, and creating computer images. The primacy of text, which Ms. McCorduck believes to be coming to an end, is neither an accident nor the result of a slavish adherence to tradition. Attention has to be paid to text because of the depth and richness of its content. No amount of speculation about virtual reality can escape the reality (called, archly, "uppercase Reality" by Ms. McCorduck) that words can store and display depths of knowledge and nuance unmatchable by still or moving images or the fake experience of virtual reality. Insofar as we continue to learn from experience, virtual reality is a replacement for real life, not for texts.

The essential thing to remember about literacy is that it is, in Oxenham's words, the "major enabling technology in the development of reason, logic, systematic thinking, and research."[15] Nothing based on sound, images, or symbols, or any permutation of them, can possibly provide a technology that is equal to the written word for those central purposes of the life of the mind. This is far from a purely philosophical statement. Modern education at all levels faces the problems of huge numbers of students, rising levels of aliteracy, and the cost of building new schools and campuses in the face of inadequate funding and deeply mistaken public policy. In Peter Deekle's words: "College teaching increasingly uses electronic technology to bridge the growing gap between an aliterate population of undergraduates and an ever-expanding knowledge base."[16] It is not surprising, therefore, that educationalists, politicians, and administrators at all levels embrace "distance learning" (that is, library-less learning) and the computer in every classroom as panaceas and de-emphasize the importance of reading and writing. Librarians should not be complicit in these intellectually lazy courses of action, but should work with their natural allies—teachers, faculty, and parents—to emphasize the importance of literacy and sustained reading to students.

Literacy—the Bottom Line

The civilization that has lurched, with many ups and downs, from classical times to the present day is dependent on literacy and the spread of literacy into the less-privileged classes. It is possible that the spread of television and access to the Net are a serious challenge to literacy and that only the privileged will be literate in the future (as was the case until the twentieth century). Libraries and librarians must do their best to ensure that we do not regress as far as literacy is concerned. We must do that by emphasizing that the sustained reading of texts is important to all of us—not least because our civilization may depend on it.

NOTES

1. Walt Kelley, *Pogo Files for Pogophiles* (Richfield, Minn.: Spring Hollow Books, 1992), 217.

2. All three definitions are from *Webster's New Collegiate Dictionary* (1960).

3. David Wood, *How Children Think and Learn,* 2d ed. (Oxford: Blackwell, 1998), 210–211.

4. Ibid.

5. Rudolf Flesch, *Why Johnny Can't Read—and What We Should Do about It* (New York: Harper, 1955).

6. Neil Postman, *Amusing Ourselves to Death* (New York: Viking, 1985).

7. Wood, *How Children Think,* 212.

8. Alan C. Purves, *The Scribal Society* (New York: Longman, 1990).

9. Lawrence Stedman et al., "Literacy as a Consumer Activity," in *Literacy in the United States,* ed. Carl F. Kaestle et al. (New Haven: Yale University Pr., 1991), 150–151.

10. Oscar Wilde. *The Soul of Man under Socialism* (1891).

11. John Oxenham, *Literacy: Reading, Writing, and Social Organization* (London: Routledge and Keegan Paul, 1980), 121–122.

12. Debra Wilcox Johnson, "Libraries and Literacy: A Tradition Greets a New Century," *American Libraries* 28 (May 1997): 49–51.

13. See several papers in Myron C. Tuman, ed., *Literacy Online* (Pittsburgh: University of Pittsburgh Pr., 1992).

14. Pamela McCorduck, "How We Knew, How We Know, How We Will Know," in Tuman, *Literacy Online,* 245–259.

15. Oxenham, *Literacy,* 131–132.

16. Peter V. Deekle, "Books, Reading, and Undergraduate Education," *Library Trends* 44, no. 2 (fall 1995): 264–269.

9

Equity of Access to Recorded Knowledge and Information

All societies should allow universal access to libraries,
so that they can help citizens to educate themselves.[1]

We must begin with the basic premise that everyone has a right to have access to library resources and services, irrespective of who they are and where and under what conditions they live. That concept is known as equity of access. Equity does not mean equality, but it does mean fairness. It is a key element in the concept of social justice—the idea that every person in society is entitled to a fair shake. In a world in which social justice prevailed, there would be no barriers to the elementary rights to which we are all entitled. In such a society all would have equal access to library resources and services as well as the universal rights to justice, medical care, employment, education, housing, free speech, and liberty that all humans have irrespective of their status and condition of life. This is not an ideal world, however, and the things that distinguish us each from the other have an effect on our use of libraries as they do on every other service that we need or want. An ideal world of equality of access is out of reach, but a world in which librarians and library users have achieved a far greater state of fairness than now obtains is by no means impossible to achieve.

Equity of access is often referred to as "unfettered access." "To fetter" means to restrain or confine—a metaphorical extension of the notion of physically shackling or fettering a human being. The metaphor is continued in the phrase "unfettered access"—that is, access to libraries and their services that is unconstrained and free. The American Library Association's *Library Bill of Rights* states, "A person's right to use a library shall not be denied or

131

abridged because of origin, age, background, or views."[2] The ALA statement may appear to be unnecessarily complex[2] but one can understand why the words "origin, age, background, or views" are there—because, in their absence, one could not deny access to a library to a naked person or one in the grip of homicidal mania. Absent such threats to life, safety, decency, buildings, and collections, no one may be denied access because of her age, gender, economic status, ethnic origin, or any other categorization that does not inhibit her legal, constitutional, and moral rights. In a modern twist to an old story, equity of access to electronic recorded knowledge and information implies that library "users . . . have a right to information, training, and assistance necessary to operate the hardware and software provided by the library."[3] This latter is not a negligible point, because it implies that librarians and staff in libraries large and small must possess up-to-date technical knowledge (knowledge that needs constant refreshing) in addition to their other professional abilities and skills. This is, almost certainly, a transitional phenomenon (but one of years, not months) because, as technologies become established and on the way to ubiquity, they always become simpler to use.

What Is the Relation between Equity of Access to Recorded Knowledge and Information and Libraries?

Libraries deal in recorded knowledge and information, but are not the only institutions that do so. The ideal is fairness in access to all forms, but we should recall that much of that access is outside libraries and not in the purview of librarians. Purchasing books, renting videos, using an Internet café, or visiting an art gallery are all manifestations of access to recorded knowledge and information. It is important that we play our part but, at the same time, we should concentrate on the aspects of this value over which we can have some control—access to library collections, resources, and services. We should also work with other agencies to promote all aspects of access because an educated citizenry requires the full range of access afforded by libraries and other cultural and commercial institutions.

Equity of access involves removing or minimizing all the many barriers to use of library resources and programs for all library users. Just as with many other contemporary issues in librarianship ("information competence" comes to mind), many librarians, educators, and others have focused the discussion on, and only on, the technological aspects of library service. President Clinton has an excellent record on educational issues but, alas, he has fallen into the same trap as many others. He stated in his weekly radio address of February 8, 1997:

> To give our children the best education, we must help them harness the powerful forces of technology. That's why we've challenged America to connect every schoolroom and library to the Internet by the year 2000. For the first time in history, children in the most isolated rural towns, the most comfortable suburbs, and the poorest inner-city schools *will have the same access to the same universe of knowledge* [my emphasis].[4]

I am sure that the president has been as misled by advisers as the general public has been by those who see electronic technology as the panacea for all our ills. I am equally sure that a cursory examination of the problem will reveal that students in poor rural or inner-city areas with no or poor library service absolutely will *not* have equity of access to "the same universe of knowledge," even if their schoolroom is connected to the Internet. Real library services and collections are as necessary to all children as are good teachers. This applies to all grades, from kindergarten students who need access to good age-appropriate books, story hours, the attention of skilled librarians, and all the other things that instill an early love of reading and learning to high school students wishing to read and do research into new topics.

Equity of access, then, means that everyone deserves and should be given the recorded knowledge and information she wants, no matter who she is and no matter in which format that knowledge and information is contained. It means that one should be able to have access (either to a library building or from a remote location), that library services should assist in the optimal use of library resources, and that those resources should be relevant and worthwhile.

I have already written of the importance of intellectual freedom to libraries. The question of access to library materials and library services is linked to that. It is important to make everything accessible to everybody without fear or favor, but it is equally important to ensure that such access is practically possible and not biased in favor of the better-off or the more powerful. Such equitable access is brought into question by some aspects of technology. For example, in the United States we are seeing a burgeoning scandal in the dissemination of government documents. It is well known that the information and recorded knowledge generated by the government is not as available to all citizens as it is to some business interests, and the excellent system of depository libraries is under challenge from some elements of the present Congress in their zeal to proceed to electronic dissemination of government documents.[5] (We should never tire of pointing out that we, as taxpayers, have already paid for this information and knowledge and are entitled to free, timely access to it.)

More generally, the idea of charging for access to library materials and library services is much more popular today. There seems to be a difference, in some people's minds, between "free" print and other materials and "cost recovery" access to electronic resources. Interestingly, many libraries still pay for electronic resources from outside their materials budgets, and that may condition their willingness to charge for what are seen as "extras" even in budgetary terms. In a world of access being limited by the ability to pay, the whole "virtual library" idea is, essentially, an elitist construct that writes off sections of society as doomed to be "information poor."

I am not saying it is inevitable that libraries that use technology intensively as an enhancement to their services are going to betray the value of equity of access. However, it is evident that there is an inherent contradiction in society's approach to the use of technology—the disconnect between the idea of technology making more information accessible to more people and the inability of many (because of who they are and their economic status) to take advantage of that accessibility. That contradiction should make us very sensitive to the idea of maintaining libraries that are freely available to all, irrespective of social standing and economic circumstances. The ideal library of the future will be one in which access to all materials and services (including electronic materials and services) will be freely available, without barriers imposed by lack of money or lack of technological sophistication. This value is especially important to those libraries (such as the one in which I work) that serve a population containing a majority of economically disadvantaged students.

Equity of Access in Action

There are many reasons why one individual may not have equitable access to the recorded knowledge and information that he or she needs. Not all library resources and services are available to all without distinction, and the factors that inhibit access vary from person to person and place to place. Even someone who is in a library physically may have barriers to her or his use that are not present for others in the same building. Not all these inequities are eliminated by technology; in fact, as we have seen in the discussion of the "digital divide" (see chapter 3), technology may itself introduce new inequities.

Barriers to equity of access may, broadly, be grouped into three categories—personal, institutional, and societal. Table 1 lists the types of barriers in each category.

TABLE 1   Barriers to Equity of Access

Personal	*Institutional*	*Societal*
poverty	location of libraries	education
physical disability	layout of library	politics
mobility	buildings	unequal funding of
level of knowledge	type, quantity, and	public services
level of education	availability of	
level of literacy	equipment	
English-language skills	helpfulness and number	
level of computer skills	of staff	

If one or more of the descriptions and states of living in the following list apply to you, you are very likely to have lesser or even no access to the recorded knowledge and information you need and to the services that enable you to use them.

poor

member of a single-parent household

live in a rural area

live in the inner city

member of an ethnic minority

have limited English proficiency

incarcerated

ailing

disabled

very young

old

undereducated

no access to electronic resources

no computer skills

no or limited private and public transportation

When we contemplate the number and multidimensionality of the barriers to access, it can readily be seen that creating equity of library access for all is a complex and extraordinarily difficult task.

Let us look at some things that would increase equity of access. The following is not an exhaustive list by any means; it contains measures that librarians can and do carry out or influence as well as measures that we cannot, and it consists of public policy and purely library steps to be taken. The list is not in order of priority or importance.

Increase the number of school libraries and of "credentialed" librarians to work in them.

Provide more equitable funding for counties, school districts, and other governmental units within states.

Offer classes within libraries on

- literacy
- English-language skills
- information competence
- computer skills

Keep branch public libraries open in rural areas and inner-city areas.

Ensure that wired libraries and schoolrooms are accompanied by personnel trained in computer skills and information competence.

Go beyond the minimal requirements of the Americans with Disabilities Act in building and retrofitting libraries, particularly by consulting library users with disabilities.

Work to remove restrictions on the library rights of the incarcerated.

Take library services to the people by such measures as

- mobile libraries
- branches and library services in "unconventional" settings, such as shopping malls, college dormitories, day care and senior centers, and hospitals and hospices

Ensure that online systems are current, accessible, and user-friendly.

Five Steps to Equity

If we are to work in a coordinated manner to reduce inequities of access on all fronts, we must recognize that individuals have a part to play, libraries and other public institutions have a part to play, and legislators and others interested in public policy issues have a part to play. The articulation of all these interests and influences will require a major and sustained profession-wide campaign that can only be led by the American Library Association. Such a campaign will be based on the simple idea that it is a societal injustice for access to library resources and programs to be conditioned on any of a variety of states of life. The potential for inequity is great and the factors that influence that potential are numerous. How can we even begin to remedy the situation? How can an individual librarian or group of librarians influence the world about us and improve access for the disadvantaged? The following five steps will set us on the path toward abolishing inequities of access.

1. Cease to take inequities for granted.
2. Understand the strengths and the limitations of technology so that we can use the former and learn to deal with the latter.
3. Understand and analyze the barriers to access and assign them to the following categories:
   - those over which we have control
   - those that we can play a role in remedying
   - those that are outside our control but which we can mitigate
   - those that are very difficult for us to do anything about
   - those that are impossible
4. Organize within our institutions and professional organizations to work systematically on reducing inequities.
5. Keep going after one barrier at a time is reduced or eliminated so that equity of access is a cardinal principle of all innovations and programs.

Stop Accepting Inequity

The first step in this five-step program is a matter of principles and priorities—and is a step that is more difficult, ironically, for those of us who work in libraries in which equity of access is of lesser immediacy. For those librarians in the trenches, faced daily with inequities, the principle of equity is an inevitable part of daily working life. A children's librarian in a poor rural area of California is confronted by inequity daily when she deals with children who cannot read, who work in the fields with their parents, who may have an imperfect command of English, or who regard a mandated trip to the library as an inconvenience. However, even university libraries, those apparent ivory towers, are often situated in far-from-affluent communities and serve the members of the wider community as well as those in academe. It is difficult for me to imagine a librarian who could function well in any library while remaining unconcerned about inequity of access. One does not need to be a revolutionary insurrectionist to advocate the removal of all barriers to effective library use.

Understand the Role of Technology

I think that, in the early days, many people, even many librarians, thought that technology would be the great leveler, that it would enable us to give equitable library service to even the most remote user, and that it would, somehow, make up for deficiencies in funding of library services to the disadvantaged. There can be no doubt that technology can help *if* the following conditions can be met:

> There is universal access to the Internet and the Web.
>
> Everyone has basic computer skills.
>
> The library that has been wired for the Net is accessible.
>
> Everyone is trained in information competence and critical thinking.
>
> Libraries can organize to provide services to the remote user.
>
> Use of technology is supplemented by other library resources and services.

The goal of putting terminals in every library and schoolroom has been embraced by Al Gore and Bill Gates and myriad lesser mortals. Once achieved, is the provision of those terminals to be backed up by knowledgeable professional assistance that is freely available? Will a schoolroom equipped with modern computers with high-speed access to the Internet compensate for a "library" consisting of twenty-five-year-old books and with no librarian? If you are a child or an older and less-mobile public library user, what good is a terminal in every library if your branch library closed two years ago? Even if there is easy access for knowledgeable users, what about all the recorded knowledge and information that is not available on the Internet? None of these questions is easy to answer, and their implications are ominous. It is perfectly possible that those who can influence public policy will simply install computers and walk away—declaring a victory and going home. How will we explain away a perfectly possible world of the future in which, despite near universal access to the Internet and the Web, levels of literacy and education continue to decline inexorably? Perhaps such a state of affairs would be *because* of universal access to the Net, not despite it. There is a natural human tendency to settle for what you have, and we could hardly blame a distant learner or a teacher in a rural school for settling for whatever can be found on the Internet in the absence of books and other traditional library resources. In addition, there is an obvious seductiveness about the clicking and flash of the Internet and the ability to download instantly what is discovered. This is especially so when compared with the more arduous task of sustained reading and the thought processes it induces. An old gibe about education—the transfer of information from textbook to notebook without going through human minds—is daily being recast as "the downloading of texts and images from the Net into term papers without passing through human minds."

I have stressed the importance of providing assistance to library users using electronic resources. Such assistance is especially important as a means of overcoming the passive acceptance of anything that is available on the Net, not least because of the lack of ability to know what is available only in books and other tangible library resources. As well as helping users in the library and in the schoolroom, we should be aware of what one writer has called "the virtual patron."[6] Hulshof points out that we have been giving distant users assistance at least since the invention of the telephone (or earlier, if we count postal reference service). However, he notes some particular and difficult characteristics of e-mail users—they expect the response to be as quick and easy as the request, they pose complex questions that require numerous e-mail interactions (a frustrating process), and they often require technical support and advice that the library or individual librarian may not be able to give. The latter may not be a simple matter of providing only library-related answers. As Hulshof points out, if access to library resources requires a particular suite of software, the library should be prepared to give advice on the installation and use of that software. Even if the library's personnel are prepared to answer any questions about software and systems, a user's level of technical knowledge may be so low as to make communication difficult or impossible. Then there is the perennial question of monetary and human resources. As remote access to library resources and services increases, so will the demands of the virtual patrons. Most libraries will not have new money for new staff to meet those demands and will be back to the same old "reallocation of resources"—another example of technological change diverting staff time from "traditional" services that may be no less important than the new service.

Set Priorities

The crucial factors in the third step toward abolishing inequities of access are careful surveying and analysis, beginning with your own library. The jargon of management and planning includes the useful phrase "environmental scan." That concept is very useful to the librarian who is serious about increasing equity of access. The problems are well on their way to being delineated when you begin by looking around your library and thinking about the factors that lead to inequity of access. It is a truism to state that defining problems is halfway to solving them, but the thing about truisms is that they are true. It is also important to conceptualize the process of delineation as a series of concentric circles beginning with issues over which the library has a high degree of control and ending with issues that are produced by major social forces and over which the library has little or no control.

INSIDE THE LIBRARY

Let us begin in the library and look at some of the intangible barriers to access for those who are actually there. I have written earlier in this book of the importance of bibliographic control systems to use of the library. Just as an up-to-date, user-friendly, internally coherent, standardized, and accessible bibliographic system is an invaluable aid to library users, a system that lacks one or more of those qualities may present insuperable barriers to effective use of the library. The library has complete control over its own online bibliographic system and, therefore, can remove or mitigate barriers in and to that system. The online system of today is also a gateway to a variety of other resources, from the relatively orderly world of indexes, abstracts, and indexed full-text databases to the disorderly world of the Net and commercial browsers. Obviously the library lacks the control over these resources that it has over its own database, but it can reduce barriers to use of these other resources by designing or deploying easily usable interfaces and "help" capabilities.

The question of access to the library's online system is also, of course, affected by the physical world. How many public terminals should a library have? One answer is: enough so that anyone can have instant access to a terminal at any time. Few libraries of any size come anywhere near that situation, and most university and large public libraries have dealt for some years with the problem of waiting lists for terminals. Now that almost all libraries are offering access to the Web, use of terminals is increasing apace, and even small libraries have to cope with more would-be users than terminals at peak times. In the possible future of libraries with wireless networks, users will be able to use portable computers anywhere in the library . . . *if* they have a portable computer. Perhaps laptops and such will become so inexpensive that everyone will own one and perhaps many different types of laptops will be able to use the wireless network. Perhaps, but meanwhile libraries will need to have sufficient terminals in wired libraries and lend our users laptops when we go wireless.

How easy is it for library users to gain access to your online system from their homes or elsewhere outside the library? This may be outside the library's control but it is hardly likely that someone experiencing difficulty in being a virtual library user is going to blame anyone but the library. Therefore, it behooves us to work as best we can to make remote access to our systems and resources as easy and reliable as possible. This brings up the important and often overlooked question of the public relations aspect of equity and ease of access. Just as a library that is closed when it is expected to be open can be a PR disaster, so can a foiled expectation of access to and ease of remote use of the library's systems.

A poor online system and a good online system to which remote access is difficult or impossible are intangible barriers to access. A library building can also contain tangible barriers, and a good survey of the physical plant from the point of view of all users can yield some surprising and correctable results. Many of the features of a modern library—braille tags on elevators, large-text terminals, wheelchair ramps, and wheelchair-accessible workstations—are among the more obvious enhancers of access. There are more subtle barriers—size and layout of furniture at service points, signs that use library jargon that is not understood by the bulk of library users, confusing arrangement of materials, poor wording of interfaces, and many others. Such things can often be discerned only by those who can put themselves in the place of all library users and see the library from all their different points of view.

That last—seeing the library anew—may be the most difficult approach to removing barriers to access within the library but it is undoubtedly the most productive. What does an academic library *really* look like to a first-generation student whose first language is Spanish? Do nonlibrarians know what to do when offered the choice between searching in "browse" or "keyword" mode? (Remember that the vast majority of library users use our systems without ever asking for assistance—even when they know they need help.)

OUTSIDE THE LIBRARY

All libraries live in specific environments—the institution or community that they serve. They also live in the wider world—the society of the town, region, state, and country in which they are situated. In an era of globalization, those societies include continents and, indeed, the whole world. There are forces in our localities, countries, and the world as a whole that influence our work and the people we serve. Some of those—for example, literacy, education, scholarly communication, and information technology—are areas in which we can exert some influence, especially if we act in concert. Others—for example, big electronic technology (Microsoft, Internet 2, etc.), the infotainment industry, and federal education policy—are beyond our powers. Still others—for example, copyright and intellectual property in an electronic age—are insoluble by anyone. If we are to work seriously and effectively on increasing equity of access, we must have the wisdom to distinguish among these types of external forces and to concentrate on those that we can change and affect.

Work Together

I am convinced that the only answer to the equity of access issue, once it is defined and analyzed as set out above, is a concerted multiyear effort in which all libraries and librarians participate. The American Library Association is in the process of formulating a plan to make equity of access the primary goal in its planning for the future. That push to increase equity will be led by ALA but carried out by individual librarians in concert with a large number of other interested parties. The campaign should deal with all the dimensions of access (technological and otherwise), should be politically smart and effective, should use all modern means of persuasion (including advertising and PR), and should go through continuing cycles of proposal, work, achievement, analysis, and evaluation. It should seek to involve librarians from all kinds of libraries, the institutions and communities they serve, and politicians and other public policy experts at all levels—local, state, and federal.

Here is how I see a campaign like this working. ALA should begin by declaring equity of access to be its major external priority. (I use the latter term as it is becoming evident that ALA must be effective on two fronts simultaneously—serving its membership and addressing the role of libraries in society.) It should follow that declaration by convening a broad-based Convention on Equity of Access to define the issues and priorities and then to work out a plan of action through a variety of librarian and nonlibrarian task forces and commissions. These latter would be charged with specific areas of inequity (for example, literacy and language skills; technology and lack of technological competence; rural library service; the correlations among poverty, education, and library use; library service to the old and the young; diversity issues). Their work product would be white papers delineating each issue and recommending priorities for action. Those would be widely disseminated and discussed in a variety of forums (town meetings devoted to specific aspects of the problem, over the Web, teleconferences, and so on). Those discussions would lead to the formulation of a grand plan of action to be promulgated by a second Convention on Equity of Access (which, like the first, would be comprised of both librarians and other interested parties). At the end of what would probably be a two-year process, ALA would have a multidimensional master plan that could be advanced on several fronts. The unwinding of the process would be accompanied by a public relations campaign aimed at communicating the enduring value of libraries to society. That PR campaign would make the point of the value of libraries at first and then build on and enhance the message by reports on the work of the equity of access campaign and the ways in which librarians are working together on many issues to bring the benefits of library service to all.

Take One Step at a Time

This proposed national campaign would consist primarily of the articulation of many local efforts in many areas. It cannot be stressed too often that, as with many other social movements, equity of access to library resources and services will be advanced step-by-step by individual librarians and libraries as barriers are identified and removed or mitigated, sometimes across the nation, sometimes as the result of local action involving very few people. ALA and individual librarians can supply leadership and a well-conducted campaign can supply inspiration, but the struggle will be most effective library by library as we work collectively and individually to reach the dream of a world in which library resources and services are freely available to all. That dream should inform all our actions, not just those that are part of the national campaign, but everything we do as librarians and every enhancement to library service that we make.

NOTES

1. John Stonehouse, "Spirit of the Stacks," *New Scientist* (March 20, 1999): 47.
2. Adopted June 1948, most recently reaffirmed January 1996, *www.ala.org/work/freedom/lbr.html*
3. Ibid., "Access to Electronic Information, Services, and Networks," 2.
4. *Weekly Compilation of Presidential Documents* 33, no. 7 (February 17, 1997): 163.
5. Nancy Kranich, "Whose Right to Know Is It Anyway?" in *Your Right to Know: Librarians Make It Happen: Conference within a Conference Background Papers* (Chicago: ALA, June 1992), 12–18.
6. Robert Hulshof, "Providing Services to Virtual Patrons," *Information Outlook* 3, no. 1 (January 1999): 20–23.

10

Privacy

What Is the Meaning of Privacy?

The word *private* is defined as "belonging to, or concerning, an individual; personal; one's own. . . ."[1] Private things, therefore, belong to the individual—they are her or his personal property. In a free society, the things that belong to you legally are inalienable and cannot be removed or interfered with without your permission. We all need privacy (a word rarely encountered before the sixteenth century) in a spatial sense and an informational sense. Our spatial privacy gives us the right to be alone, to associate only with those with whom we choose to associate, and to be free from surveillance. Our informational privacy is the right to control personal information and to hold our retrieval and use of information and recorded knowledge to ourselves, without such use being monitored by others. We also have the privacy that is embodied in the term "private property"—those things that we own, including intangible, intellectual private property. The rights to privacy that seem so obvious to us in our daily lives are not always legally guaranteed or practically achievable, particularly in today's technological context.

What Has Technology Wrought?

Technology is neither good nor bad in and of itself. Technological advance may contribute to societal progress or may be a detriment to society or may be both (just think of advances in fertility medicine in a world that contains 6 billion people) or may be neutral. It is a natural human tendency to personalize technology in general and specific applications of technology. For instance, how often have you heard someone say, "I hate cell phones"? Those near-ubiquitous devices whose misuse causes rage in American restaurants and theaters have been a boon in Cambodia and Rwanda—places in which it is perilous to lay telephone lines because the ground is saturated with land mines. The truth is that large numbers of Americans do not "hate" cell phones; they dislike the intrusive misuse of them by boors, bores, and solipsists. Cambodians and Rwandans do not "love" cell phones, but they do like the way they make communication without danger possible. It is the human use and misuse of technology that arouses the emotions, and it is the human use and misuse of technology that we should observe, study, and seek to amend for the better.

It often seems that every advance in technology exacts a counterbalancing price or detriment. There is no such thing as a free technological improvement. Possibly the most obvious price that we are all paying is the actual and potential erosion of privacy caused by the compilation of, and easy access to, large and complex databases resulting from commercial, governmental, and nonprofit transactions. The latter, of course, include transactions between libraries and library users and transactions that take place in libraries. Here are words to make us wary: "Every keystroke can be monitored. And computers never forget."[2] The same article quotes Marc Rotenberg, director of the Electronic Privacy Information Center:

> With the new online services, we're all excited that this is going to be our window on the world, to movies, to consumer services, for talking with [sic] our friends. The reality is that this may be a window looking in.

The point is that it is not technology that is the enemy of privacy but our joyful use of technology. We give away something of ourselves each time we engage in online transactions. Most people worry about the security of their credit card numbers, and reputable providers of services take steps to ensure that security. Many people worry about potential governmental and commercial abuse of the information we are required to supply by law or in pursuit of a commercial transaction. Though these are real concerns, there is a wider picture that goes beyond the economic and governmental. We live more and more of our lives online and the accumulations of data about us grow ever larger while there is an ever-increasing ability to retrieve and manipulate that data speedily. We are coming to see that the history of society is cyclical and that cyberspace resembles nothing as much as a medieval village—a place in which privacy was unknown.

Electronic technology pervades government, commerce, and many forms of social interaction. We are right in being concerned about the integrity of our personal data and should support efforts by governments and others to devise regulations and codes that limit (but can never eliminate) incursions on that data. As long ago as 1973, the Department of Health, Education, and Welfare issued a code on personal data systems based on the following (paraphrased) principles:

- There should be no secret record-keeping systems.
- Individuals should have access to their own records.
- Individuals should be able to prevent data gathered for one purpose from being used for another.
- Individuals should be able to correct or amend their own records.
- Organizations collecting personal data must ensure its reliability and prevent misuse.[3]

It seems to me that those twenty-seven-year-old principles still hold true in a very different computer world. They are even more difficult to enforce today than they were then, but they do provide the basis for humane and responsible collection and retention of personal data.

The History of Privacy

Privacy emerged as a social issue in the eighteenth century. Before then, people, even rich and powerful people, lived open lives because of the nature of society and the buildings in which they lived. Most people lived, ate, slept, played, and so on communally. Even more importantly in respect of privacy, there was little or no distinction between domestic life and work life. Reading and copying, for example, were communal activities in the Middle Ages. The concept of privacy and the solitary life of the mind came when communities and extended families gave way to nuclear families with houses with solid walls that contained separate rooms and were situated on private land. In the eighteenth and most of the nineteenth centuries, such houses belonged to the wealthy. Even then, communities persisted in the cohabitation of families and their servants. It was not until the twentieth century that the opportunity for privacy was available to the less well-off in Europe and North America. The important changes in the ways in which people lived and worked—notably the physical and psychological separation of work and "private life"—created a hunger for privacy that has been extended and asserted in a number of steps over the decades. One very important step was the publication of a paper by future Supreme Court Justice Louis Brandeis and a colleague arguing "the right to be let alone."[4] That influential paper (more than one hundred years ago) was spurred by fears of the intrusive capability of then new technologies—cameras, tabloid newspapers, telephones, and the like. Later, when on the Supreme Court, Brandeis was to argue that wiretapping telephones was the equivalent of opening sealed letters.[5] In the United States, the legal definition of privacy has evolved slowly in the years since Brandeis's plea for privacy. The important Supreme Court case *Griswold v. Connecticut* (which said that a right to privacy implicitly, but not explicitly, contained in the U.S. Constitution, underlies the right of married couples to use birth control) was only decided in 1965.[6] There are those who say that *Roe v. Wade*—the most famous case decided on the basis of an inherent constitutional right to privacy—is constitutionally flawed for that very reason. In other words, they believe that the Constitution protects only that which it lists explicitly. One could not possibly underestimate the effect on American society of an acceptance and application of that view.

There is a considerable body of opinion among constitutional lawyers and philosophers that the U.S. Constitution was framed on the basis of natural law and natural rights that are inherent in an ordered society.[7] Given that is so, it is not difficult to see that the Constitution is capable of interpretation that goes beyond the exact words of that document to place natural rights in a modern context. Privacy is, of course, one of the natural rights that was understood in the late eighteenth century. Privacy has been a matter of great weight to the individual and to society as a whole for more than two hundred years, but the right to privacy is nowhere near as entrenched in law and constitutional thinking as most people believe it to be.

Privacy remained a hot political, legal, and societal issue throughout the twentieth century and, in one form or another, is still fought over today. All social movements have been combated by, among other things, invasions of privacy. All the protagonists of the women's movement, the fight for racial equality, the struggle for literary and artistic free expression, and other such movements have been subject to surveillance and intrusion by J. Edgar Hoover and other compilers of dossiers on private lives. It would be naive to believe that such outrages no longer exist, but it would be cynical to ignore the advances in privacy contained in the law. That being said, unless we restrain the effects of technology, those hard-won legal rights are in danger of being vitiated by forces that cannot be controlled by law.

The Present and Future of Privacy

Technology, in the form of vast electronic records of online transactions of all kinds and the possibility of searching and retrieving personal data from those databases, is morally neutral. As noted before, people can use this technology for good or ill, for their own profit or in service of humanity. Our privacy is invaded daily—the task is to ensure those invasions are controlled and have benign outcomes. We have clear opportunities and dangers and should work to take advantage of the opportunities and reduce the dangers. In 1992, Columbia University professor Alan Westin published a list of ten important trends in the protection of privacy.[8] The trends, which are holding up well in a rapidly changing world, include the following:

> Personal information will be owned jointly by individuals and institutions.
>
> Institutions may use personal data only with the consent of the individuals.
>
> Collectors of personal data will issue privacy codes.
>
> Storage and use of personal data will be regulated.
>
> Theft and misuse of personal data will be criminalized.
>
> A federal agency dedicated to the protection of privacy will be established.

Many of Professor Westin's forecasts are proving to be accurate. One of them is not. It is difficult to see a federal agency of the kind that he envisages being established, not least because of the American distaste for central government oversight of personal matters. What has happened is the establishment of a seemingly ever-changing mixture of legislation, government regulation, and self-regulation. (Good examples of the latter are the various ALA policies and statements on privacy.)

A number of U.S. federal agencies are actively involved in privacy issues. They include the Departments of Commerce, Health and Human Services, and Labor; the Federal Communications Commission; and the Federal Telecommunications Commission—each addressing medical, financial, telecommunications, Internet, and so on privacy issues in a piecemeal manner. A large number of federal laws affect privacy. In 1999, the Privacy Exchange (maintained by the Center for Social and Legal Research [USA], an organization devoted to the issue) listed the following:

> Cable Communications Act (1984)
>
> Children's Online Privacy Act (1998)
>
> Consumer Credit Reporting Reform Act (1996)
>
> Driver's Privacy Protection Act (amended 1999)
>
> Electronic Communications Privacy Act (amended 1997)
>
> Electronic Funds Transfer Act (amended 1996)
>
> Fair Credit Reporting Act (amended 1997)
>
> Family Education Rights and Privacy Act (1974)
>
> Freedom of Information Act (amended 1996)
>
> Privacy Act of 1974
>
> Right to Financial Privacy Act (1978)
>
> Telecommunications Act (1996)
>
> Telemarketing and Consumer Fraud Act (1994)
>
> Video Privacy Protection Act (1988)[9]

All these are complemented by a host of regulations, court decisions, state laws, local ordinances, and pending legislation. Outside the circle of governmental action at all levels, there are many voluntary agreements between and within public sector entities (including ALA and other library organizations). It is obvious that this is a multifaceted problem—one that affects us all to a greater or lesser extent—and it is being addressed by many political and other agencies in the absence of a comprehensive public policy approach.

The complexity of the American approach is in stark contrast to the approach of the European Union, which has issued a *Directive on Data Protection* (effective October 25, 1998) that is binding on all members of the EU. This difference in approach means that there is no one U.S. agency and no single body of law that can link to the EU's legal requirement that personal data about the citizens of those countries can only be transferred to non-EU countries that offer "adequate" privacy protection for that data.

Dealing with the EU directive would, of course, be far easier if there were a single federal law and a single federal government agency to which we could refer. In its absence, the Department of Commerce has drafted a statement of principles that echo some of Professor Westin's 1992 provisions.[10] In summary, the Commerce Department's principles are:

> *Notice:* An organization collecting personal data must inform the individuals involved of what they are doing and their rights.
>
> *Choice:* Individuals must be able to opt out of their data being transmitted to third parties.
>
> *Onward transmission:* Personal data can only be transmitted to third parties that subscribe to privacy protection.
>
> *Security:* Organizations collecting personal data must hold them secure against misuse, disclosure, destruction, and so on.
>
> *Data integrity:* Personal data may only be used for the purposes for which they were collected.
>
> *Access:* Individuals must have reasonable access to the data that have been collected about them.
>
> *Enforcement:* There must be mechanisms (governmental or private) to ensure compliance with privacy principles. Those mechanisms must include recourse for individuals whose data have been misused, follow-up procedures to ensure remedies are being applied, and sanctions against organizations that violate personal privacy rights.

Given the increase in online transactions of all kinds, the great commercial value of personal data databases, and the increase in electronic technology capabilities, it is inevitable that privacy will continue to be a major issue and one that is increasingly subject to government regulation and private sector codes and compacts.

What Is the Relation between Privacy and Libraries?

There is a great difference between the passive accumulation of personal data for a variety of legitimate purposes and the deliberate, active invasion of privacy. The former has potential for abuse, the latter is abuse. To my mind, the greatest scandal of the complex of scandals (real and invented) that afflicts the political culture today is the wholesale and largely successful attack on the right to privacy. Letters are read, traps are laid, e-mails are reconstructed, bookstore records are happy hunting grounds for inquisitors, the most private aspects of lives are laid bare to be condemned and sniggered over, and the right to your own thoughts, your own relationships, and your own beliefs is trampled on by zealots and bigots. This is the world of 1984, the world of mind control, the world of mental totalitarianism. The confidentiality of library records and the confidentiality of the use of library resources are not the most sensational weapons in the fight for privacy (though I am surprised not to have read that an Independent Counsel inquisitor has been enquiring into somebody's public library borrowing), but they are important, both on practical and moral grounds.

In practical terms, much of the relationship between a library and its patrons is based on trust and, in a free society, a library user should be secure in trusting us not to reveal and not to cause to be revealed what is being read and by whom. On moral grounds, we must begin with the premise that everyone is entitled to freedom of access, freedom to read texts and view images, and freedom of thought and expression. None of those freedoms can survive in an atmosphere in which library use is monitored and individual reading and library use patterns are made known to anyone without permission. It is very important that all libraries follow a policy that ensures privacy and that they take steps to educate everyone in the library about that policy. In this context, we should always remember that most people in most libraries interact with library staff and student assistants far more than with librarians. Knowing this, a library with a privacy policy that is not communicated to all who work in the library is just as bad as one with no policy at all.

There is a sad irony in the fact that pre-automated systems were far better at preserving the privacy of circulation and use records than are their automated successors. Older readers may remember systems in which a book card and a user's card were matched for the time and only for the time that the book was borrowed. Once returned, the two cards were separated and not even Elliot Ness could find any trace of the transaction ever having taken place. Now, an electronic circulation system will preserve all circulation and use records unless it is told not to do so. Most library systems are set to delete circulation information after the materials are returned, but how difficult would it be for a skilled person to restore those "deleted" records? It seems, sometimes, that computer records are forever, if one has the skill, the desire, and the time to retrieve them. In addition, many systems choose to maintain a record of the last borrower (for convenience if a checked-in item is found to have been damaged or mutilated)—a small but significant invasion of privacy. Libraries serve communities, and communities breed gossip, nosiness, and prurience. Those who enjoy such things can easily find out who in their community has been reading about divorce, murder, diseases, dieting, dyslexia, and sexual variations. Is such a potential invasion of privacy worth the ability to track down library vandals?

Self-check

One technological innovation that is actually assisting the right to privacy is the "self-check" device. This machine enables the user to check out books and other materials on her own. I am not aware of any studies on the circulation patterns of self-check users as opposed to those who take their materials to a circulation desk (and offer it here as a good research topic for an MLS student). However, it would seem reasonable to assume that a library user with access to open shelves might feel freer to borrow "controversial" materials if assured that no one would see what she was borrowing. If this is true, such materials would go far beyond the obvious suspects—sexual content, and so on—and extend to, for example, materials on diseases, English professors borrowing Danielle Steele books, "happily married" people borrowing books on divorce, and musical snobs borrowing hip-hop records. The self-check machine, invented to speed the circulation process, may well be a signal contribution to the library right to privacy.

Privacy and Electronic Resources

I have noted before that there is a serious problem of disparity of access to electronic resources. In the words of Elisabeth Werby:

> [N]ot all Americans are beneficiaries of the technological revolution. Indeed the Internet is "one of the more polarized aspects of life today in America." [www.zd.com/marketresearch/InternetTrak98Q2IT2Q_ExecSummary.htm] . . . Among the "least connected" Americans are the rural poor, single parent and female headed households and young households.[11]

The figures on the "digital divide" vary from one survey to another, but no one disputes the existence of that gap. The public library is in a position to compensate for that gap (as are academic libraries, particularly state-supported institutions in communities that contain a significant number of the disadvantaged) by supplying free access and guidance in using that access. This means that the question of privacy and confidentiality is an ineluctable and important issue for libraries—like it or not. We provide access to the Internet because we believe in giving access to all materials, but this particular case is so important because we are providing access to a vital part of modern life. If we are to come to terms with a society in which computer skills are highly esteemed and rewarded and if we are to give access to modern communications to those who would otherwise be shut out, we will have to deal with the many consequences of that service. Privacy rights, intellectual freedom rights, parental rights, and other issues attached to Internet access are there and have to be confronted.

There are many age-old problems connected with library privacy, but electronic resources and computer systems have introduced new dimensions to the struggle for confidentiality. Anyone who wishes can monitor the use of online journals, find out who gains access to which Web pages, set up "cookies" that create caches of information on sites visited and resources consulted, and do a myriad other things. Here is a news item from *USA Today* (August 25, 1999):

> PALO ALTO, Calif. Privacy watchdogs are concerned about a "fun" new feature at Amazon.com [the online bookseller] that allows anyone on the Internet to find out what [*sic*] kinds of books, videos, and CDs employers at America's corporations are buying.

You do not have to be paranoid to wonder a little, the next time you key in your name, address, and other details when ordering a book or video, about the uses to which those data may be put. The Amazon.com feature sounds harmless (not to mention boring), but the fact is that such services accumulate vast amounts of data in an effort to maximize sales (for example, I regularly get messages from them suggesting new titles that are similar to those I have bought before). The consequent fact is that mass of data is open to major violations of individual privacy.

Invasions of privacy are often done with good intentions, but everyone knows which road is paved with those. In the electronic arena, users and librarians have to act to mitigate invasions of privacy and to be always alert to the possibilities for snooping and more sinister uses of data about personal use of electronic resources. William Miller quotes the chairman of Sun Microsystems as saying "You already have zero privacy—get over it," a breathtakingly candid acceptance of the 1984 implications of pervasive technology and a chilling indication of the attitudes of these modern robber barons.[12] If the chairman is right, then, surely, it behooves us to work even harder to preserve confidentiality at least in the area in which we work. Librarians should never agree to the loss of privacy and should work hard to preserve the privacy of the individual by enunciating principles, creating policies, and putting them into action. We need to develop more detailed privacy codes that are flexible enough to cover all kinds of library use in a rapidly changing technological environment.

Privacy in Action

The American Library Association issued an "interpretation" of its *Library Bill of Rights* that addresses these problems in very broad terms and provides what is, essentially, an overview of the issues and an ethical framework for library policies rather than specific practical steps to be taken.[13] For instance, the interpretation states that "[u]sers have both the right of confidentiality and the right of privacy" but also says that library users must be advised that those rights may be threatened by the technical difficulty of ensuring security of electronic information on use. Therefore, a library formulating a privacy policy should not look to this document for the details of such a policy. That said, the document does provide a useful beginning and the following conceptual bases for a policy.

> Each library should relate its policy to the needs of its own community and the environment in which it operates.
>
> Library users have a right to confidentiality and privacy.
>
> The rights apply to minors as well as adults.

This latter point is central to ALA's stance on filtering (the attempt to block "undesirable" electronic resources by programs—see chapter 6) in that, because minors are entitled to the same rights as adults, there is no excuse for depriving adults of access to information deemed "harmful" to minors. Some public libraries (for example, the one in Plano, Texas) have sought to square this circle by using filters on most public terminals and setting aside "unfiltered" terminals for use by adults and minors with parental permission.[14] This is a serious invasion of privacy in that no one should be forced to identify herself or himself or to use certain marked terminals to gain access to electronic resources.

The first step in formulating a privacy policy for libraries in the light of the ALA principles is to define the many issues that center on privacy. In essence, the library has to answer the following questions:

> Are circulation and other library records always confidential?
>
> Is the right to privacy different for different media?
>
> Does the age or the status of a library user affect privacy?
>
> Have all library users the right to access to all forms of information and recorded knowledge without monitoring?
>
> Under which circumstances can privacy be abridged?
>
> How far must the library go to ensure privacy?

Let me translate each of these questions into concrete (and actual) examples and essay some answers.

Q: Can law enforcement officers have access to circulation records?

A: Those records should be made available only on production of a subpoena.

Q: Does the right to privacy about book-borrowing habits extend to Internet use habits?

A: Yes, and any automatic tracking of use should be deleted or aggregated so that details of individual use are lost. It is acceptable, indeed recommended, that library use data be aggregated so that statistics on the use of the library by classes of persons (children, graduate students, etc.) can be retained and analyzed, even though the use patterns of individuals are erased.

Q: Is a parent entitled to know what her child is reading or viewing? Is a college professor entitled to know which students have checked out materials she placed on reserve?

A: The first question is tricky, but a parent who is entitled to know what her child is reading is not entitled to access to library records to gain that knowledge. The library is not a child's guardian or monitor, and parents should gain their knowledge about their children's reading habits from the children in an atmosphere of mutual respect. The second question is easy. No.

Q: Can any user of the library use any library materials and resources (including sequestered collections and Internet terminals) in privacy and without supervision?

A: Libraries often keep collections of controversial materials in supervised places for reasons of security (it should never be for reasons of morality). Access to those collections should be as freely available to all users as possible. The only reason for monitoring Internet use is in cases when a time limitation is imposed because demand for terminals exceeds supply.

Q: If a children's or school library holds a reading competition, can it publish the list of books read by the winners?

A: Yes, *but* only with the permission of the winners themselves. This illustrates the point that mutual consent is a necessary precondition of any breach of the confidentiality compact between the library and its users, even for benign reasons.

Q: Should a library install barriers, screens, and the like or special furniture (even if they involve significant expense) to ensure that only an Internet user can see what he is viewing on a library terminal?

A: Yes. Just as a library user can read any library book without others knowing what he is reading, that library user should also be given reasonable accommodation to ensure privacy of Internet use.

Library privacy plans need to be built on a combination of principle—the natural law right to privacy—and experience—the case studies that illuminate and exemplify a principle in changing and different circumstances. The example of law enforcement access to library records is a perfect example of principle and experience in balance. The principle is that library records are confidential. Experience and the greater good of society tell us that confidentiality can be breached if, and only if, a formal legal instrument, such as a subpoena, is invoked and produced. Some years ago, FBI agents interrogated a number of academic librarians about the reading habits of foreign scientists working in this country. Quite properly, librarians were not awed by the flashing of a badge and, in almost all cases, refused to answer such questions in the absence of a proper instrument of authority.

As you will have seen from the preceding questions and answers, privacy and confidentiality issues are more complicated today. The environment in which we live is one of a complex of laws, regulations, regulatory bodies, and private practices. All the more reasons why libraries, and everyone who works in them, should be alert to the right to privacy and the policies that ensure that right is assured. Before electronic technology had the major impact on libraries that we see today, privacy and confidentiality of library records and personal data on library users were relatively simple affairs. We now live in a world in which many issues connected with going online are "hot" and are affected by political and religious views. Our privacy codes need to be updated so that we can deal with modern circumstances without ever compromising our core commitment to privacy as an important part of the bond of trust between libraries and library users. That bond of trust is a precious thing and one that we should do our best to preserve. In the face of the onslaught of technology, it is more than ever important to preserve human values and human trust so that we can demonstrate that we are, above all, on the side of the library user and that user's right to live a private life.

NOTES

1. *Webster's New Collegiate Dictionary* (1960), s.v. "private."

2. Peter McGrath, "Info 'Snooper Highway,'" *Newsweek* 125, no. 9 (February 27, 1995): 60–61.

3. Department of Health, Education, and Welfare, Secretary's Advisory Committee on Automated Personal Data Systems, *Records, Computers, and the Rights of Citizens* (Washington, D.C.: GPO, 1973).

4. Louis Brandeis and Samuel Warren, "The Right to Privacy," *Harvard Law Review* (1890).

5. Cited in Frank M. Tuerkheimer, "The Underpinnings of Privacy Protection," *Communications of the ACM* 36, no. 8 (August 1993): 69–73.

6. *Griswold v. Connecticut*, 381 U.S. 479 (1965).

7. Philip A. Hamburger, "Natural Rights, Natural Law, and American Constitutions," *Yale Law Journal* 102, no. 4 (January 1993): 907–960.

8. Abstracted in Deborah Schroeder, "A Private Future" *American Demographics* 14, no. 8 (August 1992): 19.

9. "National Sector Laws." *www.privacyexchange.org/legal/nat/sect/natsector.html*

10. "International Safe Harbor Privacy Principles," draft (April 19, 1999), *www.ita.doc.gov/ecom/shprin.html*

11. Elisabeth Werby, "The Cyber Library: Legal and Policy Issues Facing Public Libraries in the High-Tech Age" (National Coalition Against Censorship), *www.ncac.org/cyberlibrary.html*

12. *Library Issues: Briefings for Faculty and Administrators* 19, no. 5 (May 1999): [4].

13. "Access to Electronic Information, Services, and Networks" (American Library Association, 1999), *www.ala.org/alaorg/oif/electacc.html*

14. *Dallas Morning News* (August 24, 1999).

11

Democracy

What Is Democracy?

Democracy is, in essence, the concept of social equality. The word itself derives from two classical Greek words meaning "the people" and "to rule." Democracy is such a familiar word that we rarely think about it analytically. It is an idea that is so deeply engrained in the minds of almost everyone on earth that it is almost heretical to question its universal applicability. The idea that the people rule is so instantly attractive that even undemocratic regimes frequently appropriate the word. Not for nothing do tyrannies call themselves "The People's Democracy of X" and, thus, pay lip service to the idea that the people are their own rulers.

Once one has accepted the idea of democracy, the questions are: Who are the *people* that rule? and *How* do the people rule? The answer to the first question is by no means as simple as it might appear. We should recall that it is only in quite recent times that the "people" who rule in a democracy are defined as all the people, and not just a group set apart by reason of their gender, ethnic origins, religion, and so on. The Greeks invented the word and the idea of democracy, but their "people" *(demos)* were a small minority of property-owning males.

As to how the people rule, in the political context that rule can be direct (absolute democracy, in which all vote on every public policy issue—which amounts to philosophical anarchism) or indirect (representative, in which the people rule through their elected representatives). Indirect democracy is much more practical in a complex world than direct democracy, but it requires a steady flow of information to citizens and for that citizenry to be knowledgeable about social and political issues. Beyond politics, democracy expresses a wide range of values concerned with social justice, the dignity and value of each human being, egalitarianism, and respect for differing ideas. For libraries, democracy is both a context and the keystone of a set of values that should pervade our activities and programs. Libraries serve democracy, not least when they are living examples of democracy in action.

The American Idea

The Unitarian minister and prominent abolitionist Theodore Parker called democracy "the American idea."[1] There are those who would say that he discounted the claim of the French and British, the first of which took the revolutionary path, the other the evolutionary path. It is also possible to argue that some other countries have more-developed democracies than does the United States in the beginning years of the twenty-first century. Be all that as it may, even its critics will concede that the United States has been working on the democratic challenge for longer than most others, and in the face of unique difficulties that are themselves eloquent tribute to the durability of democratic ideals.

Democracy's Contradictions

Philosophers know that democracy is an ideal—an ideal that contains internal contradictions.[2] Those contradictions must be understood and taken into account if such statements as "libraries are key to democracy" are to have any meaning. An ideal cannot be achieved without thoughtful, critical understanding of its underlying premises. One contradiction within democracy, noted by mathematicians and economists, is the fact that a collective preference may or may not be the sum of individual preferences. In other words, a majority of any group may have one preference but the group as a whole may have another.[3] Another contradiction is that the self-interest of individuals may make them incapable of wishing the greater good of society or even of understanding what that greater good may be. Despite these problems, even the most rigorous analysis of the idea of democracy leaves us with this (often misquoted) observation:

No one pretends that democracy is perfect or all wise. Indeed, it has been said that democracy is the worst form of government except all those other forms that have been tried from time to time.[4]

Just consider the alternatives—totalitarianism, autocracy, plutocracy, absolute monarchy, and rule by elites. Most will settle for an imperfectly achieved ideal—democracy—over any of these forms of domination of the many by the few. On the other end of the spectrum lie anarchy and nihilism, neither of which are models suited to a modern society.

What Is the Relation between Democracy and Libraries?

It cannot be denied that a developed democracy, in any country, is an idea that depends on information, knowledge, and education. The ideal modern society is one in which mass literacy and mass education combine with accessible sources of information and knowledge to produce wide participation in all public policy decisions. The United States and all other developed countries possess the *mechanisms* of such a democratic ideal—high literacy rates, diverse information channels, and comprehensive education. Evidently, these mechanisms have produced a far from ideal result. It is a sad irony that as American democracy has reached its theoretical ideal—the enfranchisement of all adults, irrespective of gender and race—it is in danger because of an increasingly ill-informed, easily manipulated, and apathetic electorate. A culture of sound bites, political ignorance, and unreasoning dislike of government are vitiating the rights for which, at different times, revolutionaries, women, and ethnic minorities fought. Libraries are part of the solution to this modern ill. As an integral part of the educational process and as a repository of the records of humankind, the library stands for the means to achieve a better democracy. The best antidote to being conned by television is a well-reasoned book, article, or other text. All values and ideas that dominate library discourse and practice are democratic values and ideas—intellectual freedom, the common good, service to all, the transmission of the human record to future generations, free access to knowledge and information, nondiscrimination, and so on. A librarian who is not a (small "d") democrat is almost unthinkable. Libraries have grown and flourished in the soil of democracy, and our fate is inextricably intertwined with the fate of democracy.

The Democratic Library

Not only is democracy the environment we need to succeed, but we should also commit ourselves to democracy within the library. That is, all libraries should be organized and managed in a democratic manner and with respect for the rights and dignity of all who work there. The "literature" of management is as extensive as it is stodgy and the theories of management are as numerous as they are evanescent. I am as heartily sick as the next person of the annual management fad to which American universities seem to be fleetingly addicted. What is striking about all the alphabet soup of management fads (MBO, TQM, etc.), apart from their barbarous management-speak and their essential similarity each to the other, is the fact that they all embody values and ideas that have been commonplace in many libraries for decades. It is always galling when it dawns on one that the jargon of this year's management fad may be different but, essentially, it is preaching the same old cooperation, tolerance, participation, mutual respect, encouragement of innovation and diversity, and so on. They always add up to what a former colleague of mine called "applied feminism"—virtues that are manifest in the democratic nature of well-run libraries.

Democracy in Action

The Library as an Integral Part of Democracy

Collectively, library collections constitute the memory of humankind. Just as a human being without memory is incapable of dealing with life, a society without memory cannot function. If, as many have said, an informed and educated citizenry is essential to democracy, it is obvious that the collective memory provided by libraries is as essential to democracy as classroom instruction, one-on-one teaching, and any of the other components of effective education. Moreover, because libraries are an important part of lifelong learning, they play an educational role for citizens throughout their lives and not just for those in formal educational programs. There is a reason why antidemocratic individuals and groups seek to censor publications and to control what is or is not held by libraries. That reason is called the power of ideas. A single thread runs from *1984* through *Fahrenheit 451* to today's books and movies about totalitarian futures—censorship as an important part of mind control. The case of Russia today is illuminating on this point. Freedom of the press and freedom of expression have characterized modern Russia's faltering steps toward democracy, after centuries of repression by tsars and commissars. They have been among the few bright features of a darkling picture, but they are lights that will continue to shine as Russia's desperate economic and societal problems are resolved in the decades to come. If they do not, then rest assured that democracy will have faltered or failed entirely. Literacy is important, but it is a tool that can be used effectively only in an environment of free expression and the widespread dissemination, availability, and preservation of that free expression. Russia has had high levels of literacy and education for many decades, but it is only the past decade that has seen the end of censorship and the free publication of ideas of all kinds. There are a number of reasons why the use of libraries rose sharply in Russia in the 1990s.[5] There is, however, little doubt that the move toward democracy and access to all opinion is a major factor in that increased use.

Knowledgeable Citizens

The nature of modern politics and political contests has made it difficult for the citizenry to come to informed and knowledgeable conclusions. Political advertising and campaigning, which, in most states, means television advertising and campaigning, is the antithesis of unbiased and straightforward information. In fact, campaigns for election and about public policy issues built on images and spin are explicitly and intentionally deceptive. They seek to present things and people as they are not and substitute emotion for reason and feelings for thought. It is easy to blame this style of campaigning and presentation of issues as the sole or most important affliction of modern American democracy. It is easy, but it is wrong. Any truthful campaign adviser or advertiser will tell you that there has to be something that is real at the kernel of what they are selling. They will also tell you that the most vigorously pushed person or issue cannot succeed unless there is some degree of consonance between the image and reality. The real danger lies in the context in which televised images and ideas are absorbed. Those images and ideas dominate because so many live in an environment of ignorance. Citizens who lack understanding of political issues or who cannot relate those issues to a wider societal understanding are as easy prey to political advertising as they are to commercial advertising.

Libraries as Foes of Ignorance

Libraries offer good information and authentic recorded knowledge as well as assistance in locating and assessing that information and recorded knowledge to all from the earliest days of childhood to the later days of life. Put simply, there is no reason for any citizen of the United States to remain ignorant of any public policy issues as long as she or he has access to a library and its services. The problem arises when libraries are underused or not used at all. It also arises when seekers of knowledge and truth substitute use of the Internet for use of the whole range of library materials. The Internet can give those citizens who have easy access to it (50 percent of the population at most) the ability to survey a number of newspapers and journals and, thereby, to read about public policy issues from a variety of perspectives. Because those newspapers and most journals are electronic versions of their print publications, the authenticity of their content is not usually in doubt. (That cannot be said about the ease with which they can be read, unless the reader wishes to spend a fortune on printing.) Once the reader leaves the newspaper and journal island for the rest of the Internet swamp, the picture changes. If one were to rely entirely on one's ability to locate quality Net resources other than newspapers and journals, one's understanding would be little better than that of someone who watched television advertisements only.

Promoting Democracy

If libraries are to combat ignorance, they must ensure that citizens use libraries and see them as repositories of democratic ideas and as central to the functioning of democracy. Perhaps the time has come for more libraries to move from passivity to intervention in politics—not in the sense of taking political sides but in supplying the information and recorded knowledge citizens need and encouraging informed and knowledgeable discussion of public policy. The library that is "the one good place in the city" (see chapter 3) can be a forum of ideas exchanged in spoken as well as written form. Such activity can take many shapes. The National Issues Forums (NIF) are a very good example of one kind of civic involvement.[6] The NIF is a nonpartisan program that organizes public policy discussions with the express aim of encouraging political participation. NIF meetings are sponsored by a large number of bodies, such as churches, universities, schools, and civic organizations. The sponsors include more than one hundred libraries of various kinds—public, state, and academic. The "town hall"–style discussions cover a range of topics, including juvenile crime, the environment, and race relations. Each forum offers participants the chance to vote in a straw poll, the results of which are collected and published by the NIF. The discussions are based on reading booklets and other matter made available by the library. In the words of the Lake County (Illinois) Public Library announcement of a forum held in 1999:

> Led by a moderator, these forums let participants voice their opinions on current issues affecting our nation. Upon registration, participants will receive a booklet developed by the NIF Institute outlining current opinions held on the issues. The booklets also contain before and after ballots that are completed by participants and sent to National Issues Forums for their yearly reports to local and national leaders . . . this way your voice will be heard! A new topic is discussed each month.

Thus, the library can not only provide space for citizens to gather but also the recorded knowledge and information necessary to fuel the discussion. As a variation on the theme, some libraries have sponsored groups that meet on a regular basis—a kind of public policy book club. Castelli quotes one library director as saying, "The biggest thing about NIF is that it's brought more people to the library and made them see it as something besides books." That library (Tonkawa, Okla., Public Library) was not only doing good work in the public policy arena but was also raising the profile of the library and the library consciousness of the citizenry. A good example of an NIF discussion and of civic collaboration was the forum entitled "People and Politics: Who Should Govern," which dealt with campaign financing, becoming politically active, voting, political leadership, and other related matters. The forum was sponsored by Cuyahoga County (Ohio) Public Library and Cleveland Public Radio and was held in the library in June 1993.[7]

Libraries of all kinds can encourage democracy using many different approaches—exhibits, lectures, teleconferences, reading lists, Web sites, and every other way in which we can help people to become more aware and informed. The Library of Congress has always seen itself as a leader in promoting education in democratic values.[8] The Harry S Truman Library in Independence, Missouri, is undergoing a major renovation and planning to reopen with, among other things, "an innovative curriculum for area young people studying how democracy works."[9] Those of us in less splendid or less specialized libraries can, nevertheless, play our part in giving access to and disseminating the knowledge and information on public issues that the public needs.

Information Policy

There have been calls for an "information policy" ever since electronic resources began to play a major part in modern life. The idea is that the government, in order to ensure that democratic values endure, should set out policies that govern the flow and use of information, particularly in electronic form. The fixity and authenticity of print publications have enabled us not only to live without any such policy but also to recoil in horror from the very idea of government interference in, and control of, the flow and use of recorded knowledge and information. The late Hugh Atkinson often observed, acerbically, that the United States once had an "information policy"—it was called the Sedition Act![10] His point was that any mechanism that allowed government to control what is written and disseminated to good ends could equally easily be used for bad antidemocratic ends, including censorship. Despite this clear and present danger, people of goodwill have continued to call for national policies that guarantee such good things as privacy, universal access, security, and intellectual property rights. These are good things (as noted elsewhere in this text) and the "information age" has changed the environment without doubt, but do we really want the government to create and enforce the rules governing what we write and read (in electronic or any other form)? One school of thought holds that such policies are going to be made anyway, so it behooves librarians to be involved in their formulation.[11] Another thinks that there should be rules but that those rules should evolve from the users of the Net themselves, without any government role in their formulation. Yet another thinks that the Net and the Web are anarchic and uncontrollable and any attempt to write and enforce rules for them is to try to catch lightning in a bottle. One salutary note—the country that has the most effective information policy in the world today is the People's Republic of China, having had great success in suppressing Internet access to most of its citizens and effectively controlling much of the external broadcasting to that nation.

The most likely outcome of all the changes that we are experiencing is that we will stumble into a variety of solutions and apply common sense, consensus, existing laws, and constitutional principles to individual cases in the electronic environment with greater and lesser success. Then, at some distant date, we will see that a set of policies has emerged without a grand plan or centralized control. My belief is that democracy is strong enough to survive the changes wrought by the proliferation of electronic communication and to absorb those changes into the warp and woof of an enduring democratic society.

Democracy and the Net

Extravagant claims were made in the early days of the Internet as to its potential as a force for good in the world. In particular, many believed that the Net would empower the individual in a corporate age, liberate the powerless living in undemocratic societies, and create a flowering of individual expression that would dwarf anything we have ever seen. There is no doubt that the Net, together with other aspects of modern technology, has made it more difficult for repressive regimes to keep their citizens in the dark. There is no doubt that those with access to the Net are able to express themselves to a potentially worldwide audience. Political activity on the Net is increasing at a great rate and any voter or potential voter with Net access at home or in a library can find information about candidates with great ease. Those who think that the Internet is a democratizing force have to deal with the fact that the political information found on the Net is no better and no worse than that found in TV political advertising and other media. Unfortunately, propaganda is propaganda no matter where it is found. As for the ability of everyone to publish her own thoughts and ideas on the Net, that runs full tilt into the problem of "data smog"—so much out there that any particular electronic document is very difficult or impossible to find. The logical and inevitable result of unfiltered Net publishing is *The Drudge Report,* an electronic newsletter of gossip, innuendo, and unsubstantiated stories that has explicitly abandoned all remaining journalistic standards. Libraries must work with the advantages and disadvantages of the Net by helping our users benefit from its valuable components while being able to discriminate in their choice of information. Democracy benefits from an informed citizenry; a misinformed citizenry damages it. We should dedicate ourselves to understanding the rapid development of electronic communication and to imparting that understanding to the users of our libraries by all the means at our disposal.

Inside the Library

As a matter of principle, libraries should be run on democratic, consultative lines. As a matter of fact, all libraries of any size have a hierarchical structure within which managers, librarians, staff, and other library workers operate. Full democracy and hierarchy are inimical. The question, then, is how can we balance our desire for democratic values and the imbalance of power and influence between the constituent groups of the library workforce? Though difficult to achieve, that balance should always be sought and should be a consideration in all policy decisions.

A library, if well managed, is run on a combination of idealism and the quest for efficiency. Unlike private business, which can concentrate on profits (good) and losses (bad) and which can direct all its effort to maximizing the former and eliminating the possibility of the latter, libraries and other public sector enterprises have more complex and sometimes contradictory aims. The desired balance can be summed up this way: "as much democratic participation as is consistent with the delivery of library service and the preservation of all our other values." Therefore, democracy as a library value can be a practical tool in, among other things,

> deciding to consult as widely as possible
>
> creating an organizational structure that is as simple as possible
>
> letting decision making reside at the lowest point in the organizational structure that makes sense
>
> empowering library workers by giving them as much control over their working lives as is consistent with good library service
>
> making sure that communication goes all ways in the library's organization—up, down, and sideways
>
> creating and maintaining many different avenues of communication
>
> working hard on the complicated demarcations between consultation, information, and participation
>
> being flexible in adapting plans, policies, and procedures as change demands
>
> never planning for planning's sake and keeping plans simple, briefly expressed, and widely understood

All these add up to a library version of participatory management—a term commonly used in writings on management and a key constituent of modern management theory. Louis Kaplan noted that participatory management is a relatively new idea in libraries.[12] In fact, the typical scholar-librarian library director of the period up to the 1960s rarely consulted the majority of his staff, still less regarded them as part of the management of the library. That has changed—more quickly in theory than in fact, but, as Kaplan notes, "Even the 'pseudo' participation practiced in some libraries today is a step in the right direction."

Participatory management evolved in the business and industrial world as part of the move toward social responsibility and the desire of workers to be treated with dignity and respect. The commitment to participation is an expression of the moral corporate culture of the company or institution and of the moral autonomy of its workers.[13] The central idea is that participation not only will make an entity more efficient and productive but also will empower all its workers and raise the level of work satisfaction.

To apply participatory management in any corporate entity (including a library), one must overcome a number of obstacles, not the least of which is accepting that its full realization is next to impossible. The anarchist communes of watchmakers in the Jura, Switzerland, in the nineteenth century may be the nearest to a totally democratic workplace and society that we are likely to achieve in this vale of tears.[14] It is not a model that we can even approach in modern society and modern institutions of any kind.

Let us see what participatory management comprises:

collegial consultation on a broad range of topics, including all important policy directions

broad understanding of policies and issues on the part of management and other workers

good communication channels and diverse means of expression

willingness to participate on the part of everyone

willingness to surrender authority and control

willingness to be accountable and accept responsibility

planning

None of these is easy to achieve and the hurdles of control and complacency are difficult to overcome. Even more of an obstacle is the fact that we all work in a hierarchy of power and pay, of powerlessness and less pay. We are all familiar with discussions that go nowhere, with communication channels that convey empty words, and with mutual misunderstanding between management and workers. There are two things that libraries can use to achieve the participatory democracy they want. The first is the extensive history of participatory management in business. We can learn from the mistakes in that history and we can learn about the limits that hierarchical structures impose on democratic ideas. Second, we can use the many positive virtues of librarians as a class—tolerance, education, openness to ideas—as tools in the participatory process.

What can libraries learn from the experience of business? A 1998 discussion of empowerment of workers in business organizations states that little growth of empowerment (a critical feature of participatory management) has occurred in the past thirty years.[15]

> Managers love empowerment in theory, but the command and control model is what they trust and know best. For their part, employees are often ambivalent about empowerment—it's great as long as they are not held personally accountable.

The article goes on to discuss the two types of commitment exhibited by employees. The author calls the typical state of affairs "external commitment," in which employees' working conditions, performance goals, and priorities are defined by others. Its opposite—internal commitment—applies to those who define their own tasks, work routines, and priorities, and who also define their goals in consultation with management. He points out that the inevitable inconsistencies between participation and lines of authority have produced contradictory programs that have made many employees disillusioned by having been told, in essence, "do your own thing—the way we tell you." The ultimate aim of any organization is effectiveness and performance, not morale, work satisfaction, or commitment. As Argyris points out, when those personal goals take precedence, they "cover up many of the problems that organizations must overcome in the twenty-first century."

The best thing we can learn is that we have to deal with balancing opposites, managing within limits, and reconciling group and personal aims. In short, we need to approach democratization of the library workplace with common sense and maturity. The first step is to come to terms with the management structure. Even after you have made such a structure as simple as possible, given the nature of the library and the limitations on the power of the management to reorganize, there will still be a hierarchy and there will still be groups in the library (management, librarians, staff) with different responsibilities and rewards. If your library is to achieve an appropriate level of democracy, those issues will need to be discussed and, when possible, resolved. There are limits on participation and it is important that they be clearly understood and delineated. The second step is to ensure that management is committed to consultation and communication and that librarians and other nonmanagement employees are committed to participation and to collective and individual accountability. The third step is to institutionalize participation and communication so that they become the environment in which the library operates, rather than an add-on in special circumstances. Last (and first), everyone who works in the library should respect and value the talents and aptitudes of everyone with whom she or he works, and respect and value their humanity, individuality, and dignity. That is the least that democracy and good librarianship demand.

Democracy within and Without

Librarians have always, knowingly or otherwise, been small "d" democrats. The idea of democracy is so entwined with all our beliefs that many of us hardly think of it and the consequences of the democratic idea. Be that as it may, our libraries are bastions of democracy in society and democracy is an important value within our libraries. Democracy needs knowledgeable citizens, and libraries are prime movers in providing knowledge and information to the citizenry. We instinctively turn to democratic ideas in how we run our libraries and cooperative library programs, and those ideas enable our libraries and programs to survive and flourish. We could do a lot worse than ask the question, What is the democratic thing to do? whenever we are faced with a dilemma in running libraries or providing library service.

NOTES

1. Speech at an anti-slavery convention, Boston, 1850.
2. "Democracy," in *The Oxford Companion to Philosophy*, ed. Ted Honderich (Oxford; New York: Oxford University Pr., 1995).
3. For example, a majority may vote for a tax cut and then lament the loss of services caused by that tax cut.
4. Winston Churchill, Speech in the House of Commons, November 11, 1947.
5. Evgeny Kuzmin, "From Totalitarianism to Democracy: Russian Libraries in Transition," *American Libraries* 24, no. 6 (June 1993): 568–570.
6. Jim Castelli, "The National Issues Forums: Promoting Democracy in Libraries," *American Libraries* 23, no. 6 (June 1992): 510–512.
7. "Nourishing Democracy," *American Libraries* 24, no. 8 (September 1993): 690.
8. John Y. Cole, "Books, Reading, and the Library of Congress in a Changing America," *Libraries and Culture* 33, issue 1 (winter 1998): 34–40.

9. Bryan Burnes, "Innovative Changes Ahead at the Truman Library," *Kansas City Star,* September 16, 1999, p. 11.

10. The reference is to the Alien and Sedition Acts passed by Congress in 1798, which, among other things, were used to suppress writings and newspapers that were hostile to President Adams and his administration.

11. See, for example, Mary Lou Goodyear and Diana Ramirez, "The Information Policy Challenge," *RQ* 35, no. 2 (winter 1995): 155–156.

12. Louis Kaplan, "A Step in the Right Direction," *Journal of Academic Librarianship* 16, issue 2 (May 1990): 102.

13. Denis Collins, "How and Why Participatory Management Improves a Company's Social Performance," *Business and Society* 35, issue 2 (June 1996): 176–210.

14. George Woodcock, *Anarchism* (New York: World Publishing, 1962).

15. Chris Argyris, "Empowerment: The Emperor's New Clothes," *Harvard Business Review* 76, no. 3 (May–June 1998): 98–105.

12

Keeping Faith

On a personal and private note, I am glad that I am most of the way through my career. What I know and love about libraries probably will not exist in 20 years. I doubt that I would have been a librarian in the world that seems to be coming.

These words were written to me by one of the most thoughtful and intelligent library administrators I have ever known. Can it be that her vision is correct? That what is true and valuable about libraries will cease to exist by the year 2020? With respect, and bearing in mind that statement was made in the aftermath of a peculiarly irritating meeting, I would say no. Further, I would say that bleak vision of libraries ceasing to exist or losing all that makes them worthwhile can only be realized if we librarians let it happen. We *can* use the positive aspects of technology while resisting the negative aspects of some implementations of technology. We *can* hold fast to our values and proclaim our value. We *can* understand the complexity and diversity of libraries and the ways in which they evolve as their users and the communities they serve shape them. As Walt Crawford has written:

> We do ourselves a disservice when we speak of "the library." There's no such thing as "the library"—there are tens of thousands of individual libraries, each serving a unique community with a unique combination of collections, resources, and services. One strength of libraries is their sheer diversity, particularly as libraries work together to meet future needs.[1]

One of the principal purposes of the examination of core values attempted in this book is to assist us, individually and collectively, to focus on the attributes and purposes of libraries that make them unique and valuable. I am convinced that such an examination of our values and purposes points to one inescapable conclusion—that libraries will continue indefinitely with their functions unchanged in essence. More, I am convinced that, if our society is to prosper spiritually, intellectually, and materially, libraries *must* continue to acquire and give access to, arrange, make accessible, and preserve recorded knowledge and information in all formats, and provide assistance and instruction in their use. Librarianship is generally viewed as a staid and small "c" conservative profession. Despite that, we are gripped periodically by fads and manias (remember "media centers" and the microform "revolution"?) of which the obsession with electronic technology is merely the latest and most blatant. In such times, it is more than ever important to keep our eyes on the prize and to keep faith with our predecessors and successors. This is by no means an easy task in an atmosphere of hype and fantasy, but pride in our achievements and value and clear-eyed assessment of where we are and where we are going will prevail. Beliefs rooted in reality and understanding always prevail over shallowness and anti-intellectualism. If we understand our beliefs and values truly, the profession my friend believes to be fatally weakened will become ever stronger. Our progress may be slow, but if we are valiant for truth, all the trumpets will sound for us.

Our Singular Value

Service is a key value of librarianship, but it is a value that we share with many other entities. *Equity of access* to recorded knowledge and information is a societal goal that we must lead in achieving, but librarians are not the only people in pursuit of that goal. *Privacy* is a universal concern, made even more urgent by technological advance. *Democracy* in library management and the struggle for democracy in the wider world are very important to us, but the whole world believes, or feigns to believe, in democracy so we are by no means alone. Librarianship is, in my view, a supremely rational profession, but all professions aspire to *rationalism*. Librarians lead the fight for *intellectual freedom*, but we have many allies (as well as many enemies) in that struggle. *Literacy* is a value of all in most societies, but it has a special meaning for us, because it is the key to the one value that is unique to librarianship. That value is *stewardship*.

Stewardship

As I have written in chapter 4, our role as preservers and transmitters of the human record is the one unique value of the eight I have discussed. This is not to say that it is the most important of the eight. Indeed, I would say that each of the values covered by this book is equally important—no facet of a gem is more important than other facets. It is difficult to imagine an effective library or a productive career in librarianship that lacks any of the eight values to a significant degree. Be that as it may, stewardship of the records of humankind is the one task we have that we do not and cannot share with others. The written, visual, and aural records of civilization come from all eras since the dawn of history; from all continents, countries, and communities; and in all formats—from medieval manuscripts to books, films, and electronic resources. We have a duty to preserve and transmit all these records—a duty that, obviously, must depend on a pooling of work in local, regional, national, and international efforts of all kinds. All these collaborations are founded on a multitude of individual efforts and commitments and individual willingness to contribute to that grand and continuing task. The ultimate reason for preserving all these texts, images, and recorded sounds is to ensure that future generations can read, see, and hear them and, in so doing, acquire knowledge so that they can generate new knowledge. That new knowledge will be, in turn, contained in records consisting of texts, images, and sounds that themselves augment the human record. Thus the unending cycle of acquiring, creating, recording, preserving, and transmitting knowledge goes on to enhance society and advance civilization. None of this would be possible without the work we do. All the work of the creators of knowledge and the preservers of recorded knowledge and information would be for naught if future generations could not decode the texts, images, and sounds that transmit knowledge. There are messages from the past (such as the Azilian Pebbles) that remain inscrutable—marks that we cannot read, images that we cannot interpret—but they are few, and almost all the messages from the past that we still possess can be decoded. If our stewardship is to be effective, the ability of future humans to read and understand the texts and images of today and yesterday is vital. This is why true literacy and the ability to do sustained reading are central to our mission.

Textual records are different in kind from images and recorded sound. It takes no skill to look at an image (though it takes great skill to comprehend all the content or artistic value of an image). Sound recordings are comprehensible— if the auditor understands the language or musical conventions—to anyone who has access to the machines that play that recording (the last is the rub for generations yet to come). Sustained reading, on the other hand, demands a range of complex and not easily acquired skills and a cultural and educational frame of reference that may not be readily available in the years to come. The question of preservation and onward transmittal of the human record (the most important aspect of stewardship) depends on our ability to be good stewards, but it also depends on the skills of the people of the future and the machines they use. Most importantly, it depends on the ability to read, to decode texts, and to understand the recorded knowledge of the past.

Reading—the Vital Skill

The importance of reading to personal development, education, and society cannot be underestimated. Apart from the odd fanatic like Raymond Kurzweil (who now, apparently, believes that knowledge will shortly be delivered directly to the brain without having to use the eyes as intermediaries),[2] most people accept that sustained reading is an important part of human and societal development. In the days before television and the other manifestations of mass culture, people in hundreds of thousands read books by then popular authors loved by all classes (the *beau ideal* being Dickens). Does this mean that the crowds that waited on the wharves of New York City for shipments of *The Old Curiosity Shop* and then wept in the streets on reading the latest installment were simply the equivalent of the massed millions that watch the Super Bowl or the last episode of a witless situation comedy? Michael Kammen draws an interesting distinction between popular culture and mass culture:

> I regard popular culture—not always but more often than not—as participatory and interactive, whereas mass culture . . . more often than not induced passivity and the privatization of culture.[3]

Dickens (a great writer by any standard) was a popular culture figure of the first order in the nineteenth century, but his books required levels of literacy, general cultural knowledge, and involvement that are higher by many magnitudes than the minimal skills and involvement demanded by today's mass culture. Reading is not a passive activity. It requires an investment of one's knowledge and understanding in order to be productive. One interacts with a complex text in a manner that is qualitatively different from, for example, mass culture television viewing or listening to top-40 radio. That is why reading and an enthusiasm for reading are among the most important gifts that we can give to children. The following is from an interview of the English humor writer Sue Townsend by Lynn Barber:

> I said something about her "deprived childhood," but she said no, in one crucial respect it was not deprived: "My parents were bus conductors, but they were readers, and that's what makes the difference. Reading gives you choices, you don't feel constricted by your class."[4]

Reading gives you choices. The world of the future will be dominated quantitatively, as is the world of today, by mass culture, but the alternatives, represented by popular and high culture, will endure and dominate qualitatively.

Libraries Have a Future

Dear Reader,

Libraries and librarians will continue to carry out their historic mission not least because that is what society and individuals in society demand. We will profit from the present debate about the future of libraries and the meaning of librarianship because a period of introspection, if limited in time and positive in attitude, brings strength. I hope this discussion of our core values contributes to that self-examination and to the resultant strengthening of our resolve and value. I also hope that we will work together to create a new golden age of libraries, not least because we will come to understand and to actualize our commonality of purpose in the midst of the diversity of our missions.

Keep faith!

Michael Gorman
Fresno, California

NOTES

1. Walt Crawford, *Being Analog* (Chicago: ALA, 1999), 90.

2. "We'll be able to send scanners inside the brain, tiny little scanners that are the size of blood cells, that will travel through the brain, through our capillaries, and actually scan the human brain from inside and build up a database that describes everything going on in the human brain. And that's a scenario that will be feasible within 25 years," interview, *Lehrer News Hour,* September 13, 1999.

3. Michael Kammen, *American Culture, American Tastes: Social Change and the 20th Century* (New York: Knopf, 1999), 22.

4. "Double Vision," *The Observer* (October 10, 1999): 25–28.

INDEX

Page numbers followed by the letter *n* (e.g., 14n) refer to notes to items on that page. Notes to each chapter appear at the end of the chapter.

Michael Gorman is Dean of Library Services at the Henry Madden Library, California State University, Fresno. He was formerly head of cataloguing at the *British National Bibliography,* a member of the British Library Planning Secretariat, and head of the Office of Bibliographic Standards in the British Library. He has taught at library schools in his native Britain and in the United States.

He is the first editor of the *Anglo-American Cataloguing Rules, Second Edition* (CLA, LA, ALA, 1978) and of the revision of that work (1988). He is the author of *The Concise AACR2* (CLA, LA, ALA, 1999); and editor of, and contributor to, *Technical Services Today and Tomorrow,* 2nd edition (Libraries Unlimited, 1998). *Future Libraries: Dreams, Madness, and Reality,* written with Walt Crawford, was honored with the 1997 Blackwell's Scholarship Award. His most recent book, published by ALA in 1997, is titled *Our Singular Strengths: Meditations for Librarians.* Gorman is the author of more than one hundred articles in professional and scholarly journals. He has given numerous presentations at international, national, and state conferences.

Michael Gorman is a fellow of the [British] Library Association, the 1979 recipient of the Margaret Mann Citation, and the 1992 recipient of the Melvil Dewey Medal.